What Others Are Saying About NAZAH

"Through the years, I have read numerous books/articles/posts regarding the Shroud of Turin, its authenticity, and the debates which it has inspired. I found this book to be the most interesting, comprehensive, and detailed analyses of the Shroud of Turin I have ever read. As a chemist and engineer, I have always been of the mind to bypass opinion in favor of true and accurate data and analysis. I found this book to abound with both irrefutable data and solid analysis, and thoroughly enjoyed its readability. This receives a rating of only "two thumbs up" from me, as I have not a third to give."

Brian Donley Worrell
Chemist/Engineer/Doctoral Candidate
in Ministry, FICU

"I have a hard time thinking of enough adjectives to describe this book. Words like amazing, astounding, breathtaking, and fascinating come to mind, and I'm sure there are many more I can't recall. The writing style and logical flow lead the reader to the undeniable conclusion that the Biblical and Hebrew evidence clearly points to the Shroud as the burial cloth of Christ. Also, I've never seen a book so well documented. Your detailed references make it clear that this is a scholarly book by one well qualified to write it."

John D. German
Prof. Electrical Engineering, USAFA
Original STURP Team member, Author

NAZAH

NAZAH

WHITE LINEN
AND THE BLOOD
OF SPRINKLING

DR. KENNETH E. STEVENSON

NASHVILLE

LONDON • NEW YORK • MELBOURNE • VANCOUVER

NAZAH

White Linen and the Blood of Sprinkling

Published in New York, New York, by Morgan James Publishing. Morgan James is a trademark of Morgan James, LLC. www.MorganJamesPublishing.com

The Morgan James Speakers Group can bring authors to your live event. For more information or to book an event visit The Morgan James Speakers Group at www.TheMorganJamesSpeakersGroup.com

Unless otherwise noted Scriptures are taken from the King James Version of the Holy Bible KJV, public domain. Scriptures marked TLV are taken from the Tree of Life Translation of the Bible. Copyright © 2015 by the Messianic Jewish Family Bible Society..

ISBN 9781683506072 paperback
ISBN 9781683506089 eBook
Library of Congress Control Number: 2017908689

Cover Design by:
Megan Whitney
megan@creativeninjadesigns.com

Interior Design by:
Chris Treccani
www.3dogcreative.net

In an effort to support local communities, raise awareness and funds, Morgan James Publishing donates a percentage of all book sales for the life of each book to Habitat for Humanity Peninsula and Greater Williamsburg.

Get involved today! Visit
www.MorganJamesBuilds.com

Dedication

To my beautiful bride of 48 years, my best friend, my number one cheerleader, mother of our four wonderful children, beloved G-Mommy to our twelve grandchildren: Mary Stevenson. Without you this work would never have been completed. Your encouragement and prodding when necessary kept me at it until I reached the finish line. Your 5a.m. challenge paid off sweetheart. God has truly blessed me with the best helpmate He ever created. Love you!

CONTENTS

PROLOGUE

The incense wafted all around him and the bells at his hem tinkled gently assuring Yahashuah and those outside the Holy Place that the Most High was pleased with the priest as he offered the sacrifice for the sins of the congregation. Yahashuah carefully sprinkled the blood seven times upon the mercy seat eastward and before the mercy seat of the ark which contained the tablets of the Holy Covenant. Afterward, he came out again to sprinkle the blood before the veil seven times and placed the blood upon the horns of the altar; at each step his sole focus was to follow the pattern shown to Moishe on the Mountain of G-d. At the proper time he removed his linen garments, now stained with the sacrificial blood of the lamb and washed his flesh in the Holy Place just as Moishe showed Aaron so many generations before. Yahashuah, like so many before him had completed arguably the most significant function given to the priests by G-d Himself: that of atonement for the sins of the people through the *blood of sprinkling*. (Exodus 25:40; 26:30-31; Leviticus 16:23-34; 17:11.)

The holy garments, the fine twined linen veil, the blood of sprinkling to expiate the sins of the people, even the tabernacle itself all followed the pattern and purpose of Hashem. As the author of Ecclesiastes tells us, "To every *thing there is* a season, and a time to every purpose under heaven." Ecclesiastes 3:1 KJV

PREFACE

In the preceding very short vignette are contained key elements of great importance to this treatise. Within this volume we will discuss the traditions, purpose and prophecies concerning the blood sacrifice and atonement for sin. For thousands of years the Torah has been a well spring of information plumbed by Rabbis, sages, scholars and even disparate faiths, cultures and nations. The sages and rabbinical scholars for generations have provided the faithful with the Talmud, traditions, mitzvahs and insights for our spiritual journey in this earth realm all based upon the Word of G-D. Even now in Eretz Israel the majority of the faithful look forward to the building of the Third Temple for the re-establishment of the sacrificial rites and also the coming of Messiah. Again, this is all according to the Scriptures.

Which brings me to a pivotal focal point for "Nazah,": White Linen and the Blood of Sprinkling. What sets the Torah Scriptures apart from every other book in history is fulfilled prophecy. Three revered figures of the Torah that have a direct link to the Messiah in the Torah are Abraham, Moishe, and Isaiah.

To Abraham, Hashem gave the promise; to Moishe, the pattern; and to Isaiah, the prophecy. Each has a distinct purpose and role to play in the fulfillment of G-D's plan for all of mankind. While the signs of the times seem to point clearly toward impending judgment, there are prophecies yet to be fulfilled and the promise of a Messianic age of G-D's rule.

In Nazah, we will examine evidence as to how all these things are connected to several Messianic prophecies which in turn are connected to an ancient mysterious linen cloth: the Shroud of Turin. The Shroud, which has repeatedly withstood the tests of science, now comes under the scholarly "microscope" of Torah exegesis.

My involvement in all these things began over forty years ago in a carpool at the United States Air Force Academy. What started as a simple discussion of faith between four faculty members: a Physicist, an Aeronautical Engineer, an Electrical Engineer, and an English professor led to what has become one of the most fascinating on-going scientific studies of all time: the Shroud of Turin. Dr.'s John Jackson and Eric Jumper (Physicist and Aeronautical Engineer respectively) became the impetus and nucleus of what would become known as "S.T.U.R.P," The Shroud of Turin Research Project. John "Dee" German (Electrical Engineer) became our self-described "resident agnostic" to ensure that the group remained objective. With an Undergraduate degree in Engineering from the Air Force Academy and a Master's degree in English, it was my singular privilege to serve as the spokesman and editor for STURP.

STURP as a group journeyed to Turin, Italy twice. First in 1977 to present a profile of research to the Italian authorities and secondly in 1978 to conduct six 24-hour days of hands-on research with the enigmatic relic. While some have suggested that

STURP was a religious group with a predetermined opinion about the Shroud, the fact of the matter is that the over forty scientists who made the trip were Catholics, Protestants, Jews, atheists and agnostics, most of whom believed that in short order they would likely demonstrate that the Shroud was a forgery. In my humble opinion, the reason the group attracted so many top caliber scientists in the first place was their determination to understand how a man could create a three-dimensional photographic negative some 600 or more years before the invention of photography.

Indeed, the incredible discoveries that really only began in Turin in 1978 continue to this day, and for the most part those who are still alive and were with us in Turin continue to try to fathom the depths of the mysteries of the Shroud of Turin. Furthermore, while there are differences of opinion about what may have caused the image on the Shroud, there was virtually unanimous agreement that the Shroud is not a fake; it is a real burial garment that contains the imprints and images of a man whose crucifixion and death is exactly the same as that described in the Gospels for Yeshua of Nazareth. In fact, at the planned dissolution of STURP in October 1981, the group put out the following stunning statement, "We can conclude for now that the shroud image is that of a real human form of a scourged, crucified man. It is **NOT** the product of an artist. The bloodstains are composed of hemoglobin and also give a positive test for serum albumin. The image is an ongoing mystery and until further chemical studies are made, perhaps by this group of scientists, or perhaps by some scientists in the future, the problem remains unsolved."[1] STURP only stopped short of any attempt to identify

1   Summary of Official Statement Issued by **The Shroud of Turin Research Project, Inc.,** (Amston, CT.: 1981)

the man of the Shroud. As one member of the group put it, there is no scientific test for Yeshua.

For my part, the journey has included the editing and publishing of the "Proceedings of the 1977 U.S. Conference of Research on the Shroud of Turin," along with three other major books on the subject before this one. Furthermore, as a Christian, I had no problem identifying the man of the Shroud as Yeshua of Nazareth. Anthropologically speaking along, as one expert put it, "...he is of a physical type found in modern times among Sephardic Jews and noble Arabs."[2] Pathologists add that he is approximately 30 to 35 years of age whose body has been crucified, crowned with thorns, scourged brutally, and whose side is pierced between the fifth and sixth ribs. Additionally, the man's body, despite showing evidence of rigor mortis somehow left the cloth without any evidence of rot or decay. And in an as yet undiscovered process, the body managed to create a picture perfect photographic negative encoded with three-dimensional information that resides strictly in the upper curved surface of the fibers of the threads themselves. During the years of analysis and collation of the data we collected in Turin, I made my first foray into the Shroud's Jewish purview. Given that all the evidence suggested Yeshua of Nazareth as the most likely man in the Shroud I wanted to know if the burial matched Jewish customs. According to the Gospel of John, the burial of Yeshua *did*.

John 19:40 "Then took they the body of Yeshua, and wrapped it in linen with the spices, as is the Jewish burial custom." TLV

---

2   Carlton Coon, as quoted in Robert Wilcox, **Shroud**, (New York: Bantam Books, 1978) pp. 130-133

Some interpreted this type of burial preparation as a mummy wrapping. Fortunately, I was able to locate the late Rabbi Eliezer Urbach, founder of the American Board of Missions to the Jews (now Chosen People Ministry), to help resolve the issue. He made it clear that the rather simple burial indicated by the Shroud was in keeping with Jewish custom, and also offered explanations for the presence of objects that were seen on the 3-D image. A box-like object on the forehead was likely a phylactery and objects on the eyes coins, both allowed by the *Code of Law*.

In short, given all the information that we do know, this cloth points to one person in history: Yeshua of Nazareth. However, I was not prepared for the vitriol that greeted such a conclusion. Perhaps Yves Delage, a professed agnostic who studied the photographic evidence alone, reached the same conclusion and encountered similar hostility said it best: "A religious question has been needlessly injected into a problem which in itself is purely scientific, with the result that feelings have run high, and reason has been led astray. If, instead of Christ, there were a question of some person like a Sargon, an Achilles or one of the Pharaohs, no one would have thought of making any objection...I have been faithful to the true spirit of science in treating this question intent only on the truth, not concerned in the least whether it would affect the interests of any religious party...I recognize Christ as a historical personage and I see no reason why anyone should be scandalized that there still exist material traces of his earthly life."[3]

When National Geographic covered the STURP research in a beautiful article, my name was deliberately left out by the editor Kenneth Weaver, even though every bit of information for the article came through me as the team spokesman. Weaver said

---

3   Yves Delage, quoted by Ian Wilson, **The Shroud of Turin**, (New York: Doubleday, 1978) pp.20

to me, "You're a Christian and therefore not objective!" My answer was, "What makes an atheist or agnostic any more objective about their beliefs or lack thereof?" Perhaps the most unexpected source of criticism was from other believers whose responses ranged from a dismissive, "Oh, that's just another Catholic relic and probably a fake," to ad hominem attacks on anyone who could possibly believe in the authenticity of the Shroud.

Then in 1981, as STURP prepared to host a conference to announce the conclusions of the three and one-half years of intense research, I was contacted by Dr. Gary Habermas. During the defense of his PhD dissertation on Extra Biblical Evidence for the Resurrection, one of the team, a Professor who was Jewish, told him that his very thorough research had left out the most powerful piece of all: the Shroud of Turin. After a long talk, we agreed to meet and to collaborate on a comprehensive book on the subject. *Verdict on the Shroud* was the result. When a costly lawsuit attempted to stop *Verdict* based upon a fabricated assertion about the book, it almost caused me to totally walk away from the subject. I was so disheartened how something that, in my opinion, was such a potentially powerful life changing revelation for humanity was just dismissed out of hand. Furthermore, that men who had worked so closely together to arrive at the truth could so quickly be turned against a fellow researcher. Two unrelated events not only kept me involved, but gave me the determination to do all I could to get the whole truth out and make it public. First of all, when the lawsuit was dismissed by the judge who stated, "If I had read this book first, you would never even have gotten an injunction…," I took my family on a short vacation just to clear my head. Along the way, my wife Mary suddenly surprised me with a statement that sparked deeper and deeper studies into the Shroud's connections in the Hebrew Scriptures. "Honey, I think the Lord would have you to study Isaiah 52." While I knew the book of Isaiah to be very Messianic in its content, and told this to my wife, I still was not prepared for what I found as I began to study.

> Isaiah 52:13–15 "Behold, my servant shall deal prudently, he shall be exalted and extolled, and be very high. As many were astonied at thee; his visage was so marred more than any man, and his form more than the sons of men: So shall he sprinkle many nations; the kings shall shut their mouths at him: for *that* which had not been told them shall they see; and *that* which they had not heard shall they consider.

I immediately thought of the Apostle Paul (formerly Saul) standing before two kings and telling them how they KNEW these things.

> Acts 26:23–29 "That the Messiah was to suffer and that, being first to rise from the dead, He would proclaim light both to our people and to the nations. As Paul was thus making his defense, Festus says with a loud voice, "You're crazy, Paul! Your great learning is driving you insane!" But Paul declares, "I am not insane, most noble Festus! Rather I am speaking the sober truth. For the king knows about these things, and I speak freely to him, since I am convinced that none of these things escape his notice—for this was not done in a corner. King Agrippa, do you believe the Prophets? I know that you do believe!" Agrippa said to Paul, "In a short time you are trying to persuade me to be Messianic!" And Paul said, "Whether short or long, I would pray to God that

not only you, but also all who hear me today would be such as I am—except for these chains!'" TLV

If the kings of Paul's generation knew what future kings would see, something they had "never been told?", what could it possibly be and more importantly HOW would they "see" it?

Later, I met with the late Fr. Peter Rinaldi, co-founder of the Holy Shroud Guild, without whom STURP might never had gotten our collective feet in the door at Turin. Fr. Rinaldi had asked me for copies of my book to hand deliver to the Pope himself. When we discussed some of the things I had been through, he told me softly and sincerely, "Ken, when you take up the cause of the Holy Shroud, you take up the Cross."

In the pages that follow, I plan to cover not only my over forty year history of study into the Shroud of Turin, but to make a case for what I believe is the hidden purpose of the Shroud. The Shroud, in my opinion, has a purpose that follows the Biblical pattern, a purpose that fulfills the promise of G-d, and a purpose that confirms the prophecy. A purpose so timely, and so potentially pivotal that if I am correct it could only come from the Hand of the Most High.

Shalom in Mashiach

Dr. Kenneth Stevenson

PATTERNS AND
TRADITIONS

Exodus 25:40 "And look that thou make *them* after
their pattern, which was shewed thee in the mount."

"Tradition, tradition, tradition...the Papa, the Papa,
tradition..." Tevye: *Fiddler on the Roof*

Patterns and traditions play a vital role in the religious culture
and way of life that is Judaism. When I first began looking
into the Jewish connections to the Shroud it was specifically
to answer one question: did the Shroud of Turin line up with
Jewish burial customs or not?

As the incredible three-dimensional image of the Shroud
began to reveal even more information than the negative had in
the past, certain anomalies raised that very question to another

level. There appeared to be nearly circular objects resting upon the eyelids and a strange box shaped artifact on the forehead. To begin with, according to the Gospel of John, Jesus of Nazareth (Yeshua) was buried in a manner consistent with Jewish customs or traditions.

John 19:40 "Then took they the body of Yeshua and wrapped it in linen with spices, as is the Jewish burial custom." TLV

Clearly, the Shroud, as known already, did not agree with the *tradition* of some Christian theologians that the term "wound" (deo: A primary verb; to *bind* (in various applications, literally or figuratively): to bind, be in bonds, knit, tie, wind) meant that Yeshua was wrapped like a mummy. In addition, in the Synoptic Gospels: Matthew, Mark and Luke, the term cited in all accounts is "wrapped." In Luke: (eneileo: to *enwrap*: wrap in); while in Matthew and Mark: (entulisso: to *entwine*, that is, *wind* up in: wrap in (together). Both using the same root word (heilisso: to *coil* or *wrap*:—roll together).

In addition, the Synoptics all refer to Joseph wrapping Yeshua in a "linen cloth" (sindon: bleached *linen* (the cloth or a garment of it); (fine) linen (cloth). John, on the other hand, uses the plural phrase "linen clothes" (othonion: a presumed derivative of G3607; a linen *bandage*; linen clothes.) The derivative referred to here is: (othone: a *linen* cloth, that is (especially) a *sail: sheet*).

At this juncture it helps to look at another prominent Jewish burial found again in John's Gospel.

John 11:44 "And he that was dead came forth, bound hand and foot with grave clothes: and his face was bound about with a napkin. Jesus saith unto them, Loose him, and let him go."

In this case we are at the scene in which Yeshua raises Lazarus from the dead. The same word "*deo*" is in this case translated "bound" rather than "wound" as in John with specific reference to the hands and feet. Lazarus is "bound" in "grave clothes:" (keiria" a *swathe*, that is *winding sheet*: grave clothes). Furthermore, there is reference to a face cloth: (soudarion: a *sudarium* (*sweat cloth*), that is, *towel* (for wiping the perspiration from the face, or *binding the face of a corpse*): handkerchief, napkin.) The same word *soudarion* is used at the scene of the empty tomb.

John 20: 6–7 "Then cometh Simon Peter following him, and went into the sepulcher, and seeth the linen clothes lie, and the napkin, that was about his head, not lying with the linen clothes, but wrapped together in a place by itself."

We now have two burials: that of Lazarus and Yeshua. Both involve more than one piece of linen cloth in which the bodies are wrapped in some fashion, and while different terms are used to describe the linens themselves, it stands to reason that if both comported with Jewish burial customs and traditions then they would both match in specifics as well.

Most importantly at this point, we note that Lazarus is able to "come forth" (exerchomai: to *issue* (literally or figuratively): come (forth, out), depart (out of), escape, get out, go (abroad, away, forth, out, thence), proceed (forth), spread abroad) under his own power. The Greek language is so clear in this case that the translators who extrapolate to a mummy wrap burial, hasten to add that the miracle of the resurrection of Lazarus also included a miracle of loosening his feet to enable him to walk. Yet the text itself states his feet were still bound. The need for a second miracle then would be based solely on how the translators assumed that the body was interred.

Armed with this information and photos of the Shroud, along with photos of the three-dimensional images, I took a trip to Denver, Colorado an hour away to visit with Rabbi Eliezer Urbach, founder of the American Board of Missions to the Jews (now known as Chosen People Ministries). Rabbi Eliezer, a Holocaust survivor from Poland and a believer in Yeshua as Messiah was in every other aspect an Orthodox Jew, and therefore the perfect person to address the issues that needed resolving concerning Jewish burial customs. Not only did he confirm that the Shroud indeed conformed to Jewish burial customs but he pointed me to an invaluable source for further research into the matter: The Code of Jewish Law. There was a wealth of confirmation to be found in The Code of Jewish Law, which supported the contention that the burial of the man of the Shroud was in keeping with Jewish burial rites just as John's Gospel had said of Yeshua. In chapter 194, the eyes of the deceased are closed according to Genesis 46:4. Chapter 197 declares clearly to "…make the shrouds of fine white linen, *to indicate our belief in the resurrection.*" (Emphasis added). In the same chapter it states, "…if his body is bruised and blood flowed from the wound, and there is apprehension that his lifeblood was absorbed in his clothes, he *should not* be ritually cleansed, but interred in his garments and shoes. *He should be wrapped in a sheet…we are only concerned with the blood which one loses while dying, for it is likely that this is his lifeblood, or it is possible that lifeblood was mixed with it…ornamental objects*

which are attached to the corpse...must be interred with the body..." (Emphasis added)[4]

Clearly the man of the Shroud was covered with his lifeblood and was wrapped in a "sheet." In my opinion, it is the "sindon" of the synoptics or the "othone" of John's Gospel as described in the Code of Law.

Chapter 198 states, "It is not allowed to let the body of the dead remain overnight..." per Deuteronomy 21:23.[5]

> Deuteronomy 21:22–23 "...and if a man have committed a sin worthy of death, and he be to be put to death, and thou hang him on a tree: His body shall not remain all night upon the tree, but thou shalt in any wise bury him that day; (*for he that is hanged is accursed of God;**) that thy land be not defiled, which the LORD thy God giveth thee *for* an inheritance."

> (*We will see how Paul, a protégé of Gamaliel addresses this curse clearly in the chapter "A Rabbi Named Saul.")

This detail, while not specifically tied to the Shroud itself, is confirmed in all four Gospels in that Joseph of Arimathea begs Pilate to retrieve the body of Yeshua before nightfall. Furthermore, Rabbi Urbach suggested that the objects on the eyes could indeed be coins or fragments of pottery used to keep the eyes shut in death. As to the box on the forehead he suggested the Jewish "tefillin."

---

4   Gansfried-Goldin, **Code of Jewish Law**, (New York: Hebrew Publishing Co., 1961) pp. 89-91

5   IBID Chapter 3

Tefillin are two small black boxes with black straps attached to them; Jewish men are required to place one box on their head and tie the other one on their arm each weekday morning. *Tefillin* are biblical in origin, and are commanded within the context of several laws outlining a Jew's relationship to God. "And you shall love the Lord your God with all your heart, with all your soul, and with all your might. Take to heart these instructions with which I charge you this day. Impress them upon your children. Recite them when you stay at home and when you are away, when you lie down and when you get up. Bind them as a sign on your hand and let them serve as a frontlet between your eyes" (Deuteronomy 6: 5–8)…the words of the Torah are to be inscribed on a scroll and placed directly between one's eyes and on one's arm. *Tefillin* are wrapped around the arm seven times, and there are straps on the head…The word *Tefillin* is commonly translated as "phylacteries," though the Hebrew term is more often used. I have never met a Jew who puts on *Tefillin* who calls them "phylacteries"…*Tefillin* are worn each weekday morning…Among observant Jews, *Tefillin* is a *mitzvah* of the greatest significance."[6]

Yeshua was taken as he prayed in the Garden of Gethsemane. Furthermore, he was mocked by both Romans and the Sanhedrin Council, for daring to state that he was indeed the promised Messiah of Israel (Matthew 27:39–47; Mark 15:29–35; Luke 23:35–37).

Interestingly enough, it was Rabbi Urbach who first mentioned the Tefillin on the arm which would have been exactly where the fire of 1532 left a large hole on the Shroud that was patched by the nuns who cared for the cloth at that time. Moreover, he also noted that the wrappings on the arm could indeed match the broken blood flow, which appears on only arm of the man of the Shroud. Furthermore, the blood flow on the forehead could actually be following the embossed Hebrew letter "Shin" found on Tefillin to this day and standing for Divine Power as it represents two of the Names for G-d, and also indicating prayer as symbolized by Moishe holding up his hands in prayer to Hashem (Wisdom of the Hebrew Alphabet).

Tefillin

After 38 years of study and research I am convinced of that identification because of the prophetic significance of the "blood" covering the "law." As I described in the Prologue, the pattern shown to Moishe was for the priest dressed in linen garments to sprinkle blood upon the mercy seat and the altar for the expiation of the sins of the people, then he was to remove the blood stained garments and leave them (Leviticus 16–17). This pattern is discussed by the Apostle Paul (formerly Saul) in his letter to the Hebrews. Paul, a Pharisee and protégé of Gamliel, had vigorously persecuted the Church before his conversion. But in writing to his own people, about how Yeshua fulfilled prophetic Scriptures Paul makes a clear statement concerning the pattern of "sprinkled blood" for the forgiveness of sins.

Hebrews 9:6–27 "Now with these things prepared this way, the kohanim do continually enter into the outer tent while completing the service but into the inner, once a year, the Kohen gadol alone—and not without blood which he offers for himself and for the unintentional sins of the people. By this the Ruach ha-Kodesh makes clear that the way into the Holiest has not yet been revealed while the first tent is still standing. It is a symbol for the present time. Accordingly, gifts and sacrifices are being offered that cannot make the worshiper perfect with respect to conscience. These relate only to food and drink and various washings—regulations for the body imposed until a time of setting things straight.

Redemption through the Blood of Messiah

But when Messiah appeared as Kohen Gadol of the good things that have now come, passing through the greater and more perfect Tent not made with hands (that is to say not of this creation), He entered into the Holiest once for all—not by the blood of goats and calves but by His own blood, having obtained eternal redemption. For if the blood of goats and bulls and the ashes of a heifer sprinkling those who have been defiled sanctify for the cleansing of the flesh, how much more will the blood of Messiah—who through the eternal Spirit offered Himself without blemish to God—cleanse our conscience from dead works to serve the living God? For this reason He is the mediator of a new covenant, in order that those called may receive the promised eternal inheritance—since a death has taken place that redeems them from violations under the first covenant under the first covenant. For where there is a covenant, the death of the one who made it must be established. For a covenant is secured upon the basis of dead bodies, since it has no strength as long as the one who made it lives. That is why not even the first covenant was inaugurated without blood. For when every commandment had been spoken by Moses to all the people according to the Torah, he took the blood of the calves and goats, with water and scarlet wool and hyssop, and he sprinkled both the book itself and all the people. He said, "This is the blood of the covenant which God commanded you." And in the same way, he sprinkled the tabernacle and all the vessels of the ministry with the blood. And nearly everything is purified in blood according to the Torah, and apart from the shedding of blood there is no forgiveness. Therefore it was necessary for the replicas of these heavenly things to be purified with these sacrifices— but the heavenly things themselves with better sacrifices than these. For Messiah did not enter into Holies made with hands—counterparts of the true things—but into heaven itself, now to appear in God's presence on our behalf. And He did not offer Himself again and again—as the kohen gadol enters into the Holy of Holies year after year with blood that is not his own." TLV

As we will discuss in depth in the chapter on the Shroud and Prophecy, most of the significant events in the life of Yeshua involved the fulfillment of Scripture and Jewish traditions. Therefore, it should come as no surprise that the same pattern would emerge in regard to his death and burial.

There is, however, one other significant pattern to discuss before we move on and it involves a specific part of a traditional Seder: the *breaking of the middle matzah*. During the traditional Seder meal, the middle matzah is broken and a part is shared around the table. The other part is hidden away in a *linen bag*, often referred to as a *"unity"* to be found or ransomed as "afikomen" at the end of the meal. Yeshua, according to the Gospels, said the following at the Passover meal with his disciples:

> Luke 22:14–20 "When the hour came, Yeshua reclined at table, and the emissaries with Him. And He said to them, "I have eagerly desired to eat this Passover with you before I suffer. For I tell you, I will never eat it again until it is fulfilled in the kingdom of God." And when He had taken a cup and offered the bracha, He said, "Take this and share it among yourselves. For I tell you that I will never drink of the fruit of the vine from now on, until the kingdom of God comes." And when He had taken matzah and offered the bracha, He broke it and gave it to them, saying, "This is My body, given for you. Do this in memory of Me." In the same way, He took the cup after the meal, saying, "This cup is the new covenant in My blood, which is poured out for you." TLV

His broken body, like the broken matzah of the Seder meal, would then be placed in a linen shroud, stained with his blood and interred in a borrowed tomb, waiting to be anointed when the Sabbath was complete. Another Passover tradition is Karpas: the dipping of vegetables (parsley or celery) into salt water at the beginning of the Seder. The reason given most often is to remind the celebrants of the tears shed from bitter bondage in Egypt. Some commentaries also mention dipping the hyssop into the blood to mark the doors for protection from the "death angel." Those who do, also connect it to the rite of Mezuza on the door. Karpas itself is only mentioned one time in Scripture, Esther 1:6, where it is derived from the Persian word "kirpas" meaning "white linen." (See White Linen) Haggadah commentary says this connects Purim to Pesach.

The Shroud demonstrably follows patterns and traditions from priestly Temple rituals, to prayer customs, funeral rites and even Passover observances. At this point we have only begun to scratch the surface, but let's move on to Messianic Prophetic fulfillment.

THE MESSIAH,
THE SHROUD AND
FULFILLED PROPHECY

John 5:39 "Search the scriptures; for in them ye
think ye have eternal life: and they are they which testify of
me."

In the early '70s, as a new believer, I began to read much that pertained to Christian Apologetics. Due to my educational experiences, particularly at the Air Force Academy, I was determined to be able to articulate my faith intellectually. "Evidence That Demands A Verdict," by Josh McDowell became a trusted resource that served me well over the years. It was particularly effective when Cadets joined us in our home for bible study, because it offered answers to many of the questions I myself had as a cadet concerning faith.

When I began studying the Shroud in depth, one quote in particular from that book sparked my curiosity. McDowell quoted Peter Stoner in "Science Speaks," "Let's go directly to the source." Using the same John 5:39 quotation, Stoner states the following: **THE WORD** "Scriptures" in this passage refers to the Old Testament. Christ is saying that in the Old Testament we will find the prophecies referring to Himself. It is therefore in these prophecies, and their fulfillment, that we may look if we wish to find evidence that Christ is the Messiah, the Son of God, the Savior of Mankind, and everything else which was prophesied of Him, and which He claimed to be. If we find these prophecies to be fulfilled in Christ, we will establish not only that Christ is the Messiah predicted in the Old Testament, but also that those prophecies were given by God Himself. For if they were not given by God, no man would have fulfilled any number of them…"[7]

Stoner goes on to select eight specific prophecies, some of which we will use also. He then, very logically, calculates the probability of any other man in history fulfilling all eight at 1 in 10^{17}. "…we find that the chance that any man might have lived down to the present time and fulfilled all eight prophecies is 1 in 10^{17}. Let us try to visualize this chance. If you mark one of ten tickets, and place all of the tickets in a hat, and thoroughly stir them, and then ask a blindfolded man to draw one, his chance of getting the right ticket is one in ten. Suppose that we take 10^{17} silver dollars and lay them on the face of Texas. They will cover all of the state two feet deep. Now mark one of these silver dollars and stir the whole mass thoroughly, all over the state. Blindfold

---

7   Peter Stoner, **Science Speaks**, (Chicago: Moody Press 1944), -Revised Online edition 2002 Chapter 3:

a man and tell him that he can travel as far as he wishes, but he must pick up one silver dollar and say that this is the right one. What chance would he have of getting the right one? Just the same chance that the prophets would have had of writing these eight prophecies and having them all come true in any one man, from their day to the present time, providing they wrote using their own wisdom."[8]

How many prophecies are visibly fulfilled on the Shroud, and would that strengthen even more the case for authenticity? We will use the estimates that Stoner uses for prophecies that can be found on the Shroud. For those he does not, we will attempt conservative numbers according to the principles in Stoner's treatise. See if you agree.

1) "And one shall say unto him, what are these wounds in thine hands? Then he shall answer, those with which I was wounded in the house of my friends" (Zechariah 13:6). Yeshua was betrayed by Judas, one of his disciples, causing him to be put to death, wounds being made in his hands. Note the wounds in his hands. They calculate 1×10^3.

---

8   IBID Chapter 3

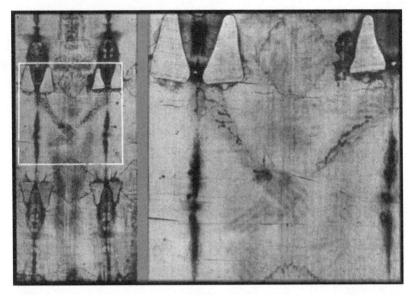

Wrists

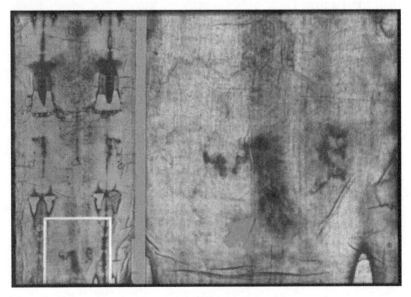

Feet

The placement of the wounds, unlike Christian tradition, is near or in the wrist, and not the palms. Anatomically, the wrist is perhaps the only area capable of supporting the full weight of the body. Furthermore, the force required to pull on those nails in order to raise the body up and breathe would surely tear through the palms. Scripturally the word used for hand is "yad" and it includes the wrist. BDB Definition: 1) hand, 1a) hand (of man), 1b) strength, power (figuratively), 1c) side (of land), part, portion (metaphorically (figuratively), 1d) (various special, technical senses), 1d1) sign, monument, 1d2) part, fractional part, share, 1d3) time, repetition, 1d4) axle-trees, axle, 1d5) stays, support (for laver), 1d6) tenons (in tabernacle), 1d7) a phallus, a hand (meaning unsure), 1d8) wrists.

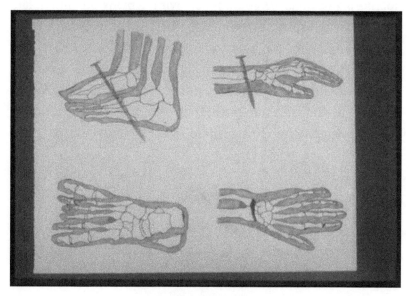

Piercing Diagram

2) "For dogs have compassed me: the assembly of the wicked have inclosed me: they pierced my hands and my feet"

(Psalms 22:16). So our question is: One man in how many, from the time of David on, has been crucified? After studying the methods of execution down through the ages and their frequency, the students agreed to estimate this probability at one in 10,000 or 1 in 10^4, which we will use. The Persians in 519BC invented crucifixion as a death form, long after David penned these words. The Romans who crucified many Jews perfected it, but as we shall see none in which all of the things seen on the Shroud were typically done.

3) "I gave my back to the smiters, and my cheeks to them that plucked off the hair: I hid not my face from shame and spitting" (Isaiah 50:6). Scourging, of the type visible on the Shroud, was a form of capital punishment in and of itself. It was not normally done in conjunction with crucifixion, but Pilate did not want to crucify Yeshua, as the Gospel narratives make clear. Traditionally, the beard of a person was plucked out when they were accused of blasphemy. The scourge wounds are one of the most disturbing aspects concerning the suffering depicted on the Shroud and there are possibly two gaps in the beard which indicates hair is missing from those areas.

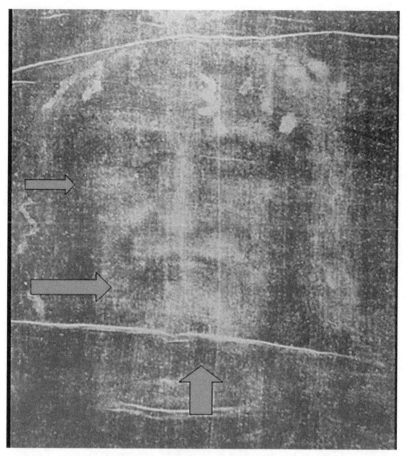

Facial Cheeks and Hair

Matthew 26:65-68 "Then the kohen gadol tore his clothes and said, "Blasphemy! Why do we need any more witnesses? Look, you've heard the blasphemy. What's your verdict?" "Guilty," they answered. "He deserves death!" Then they spat in His face and pounded Him with their fists. Others slapped Him and demanded, "Prophesy to us, you Messiah! Which one hit you?" TLV

Blood Image

With the combination of scourging and evidence of blasphemy added to the crucified it does not seem too high to again estimate the probability of 1 in 10^4.

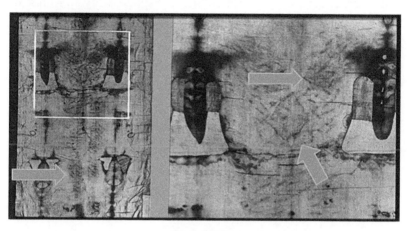

Scourging

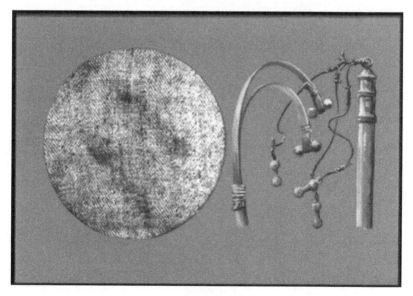

Flagrum

4) "And he made his grave with the wicked, and with the rich in his death; because he had done no violence, neither was any deceit in his mouth" (Isaiah 53:9). This man suffered a criminal's death just as recorded of Yeshua, but was apparently laid to rest in an expensive linen shroud.

> Matthew 27:57 "Now when it was evening, there came a rich man from Arimathea, named Joseph, who had become a disciple of Yeshua." TLV

> Mark 15:46 "And he bought fine linen, and took him down, wrapped him in the linen, and laid him in a sepulcher which was hewn out of a rock, and rolled a stone unto the door of the sepulcher."

> John 19:39–42 "Nicodemus, who had first visited Yeshua at night, also came bringing a mixture of myrrh and aloes, about a hundred pounds. Then they took the body of Yeshua and wrapped it in linen with the spices, as is the Jewish burial custom. Now in the place where He was executed, there was a garden. In the garden was a new tomb where no one had yet been buried. Because it was the Jewish Day of Preparation and the tomb was nearby, they laid Yeshua there." TLV

Here again we have a very unique set of circumstances evidenced by the Shroud and prophesied about the Messiah. Matthew points out that Joseph was rich and purchased "fine linen." Textile experts who have examined the Shroud agree it would have been a costly piece even back in the time of Yeshua. Also it is likely that a hundred pounds of myrrh and aloes was costly. Finally, the new tomb had never been used. Three of the four factors here are confirmed by the Shroud: 1) a criminal's execution 2) a costly burial 3) the Shroud still has the aroma of myrrh. (While no myrrh residue was detected by STURP in 1978, the aroma of myrrh was unmistakable in my opinion: a smell I have known since childhood from my Catholic background.) As most crucifixion victims were left to rot or thrown into a common pit rather than attended to in such fashion, we will stay with the conservative figure of 1 in 10^4.

5) Psalms 22:14–15 "I am poured out like water, and all my bones are out of joint: my heart is like wax; it is melted in the midst of my bowels. My strength is dried up like a potsherd; and my tongue cleaveth to my jaws; and thou hast brought me into the dust of death." David wrote that Psalm nearly 600 years before the Persians invented crucifixion as a death form, but it is an excellent description of what the crucified would experience. Psalm 22 also predates Hippocrates, the father of medical science by at least 500 years. Furthermore, prior to Yves Delage and Pierre Barbet, there is no detailed understanding of the pathology connected with crucifixion as a death form, yet the Shroud as many medical doctors attest is accurate enough to allow a "virtual autopsy." Crucifixion is an agonizingly slow form of death by suffocation. The arms of the victims are nearly pulled out of their sockets. As they hung there they would find it very difficult to breathe. With the rib cage collapsed around the lungs it would require pushing up on the nails in your feet and pulling up on the nails in your hands in order to exhale properly. Crucifixion also causes extreme dehydration. The swollen abdomen visible on the Shroud is another confirmation that the man on the Shroud suffered in exactly that way. We will again use 1 in 10^4.

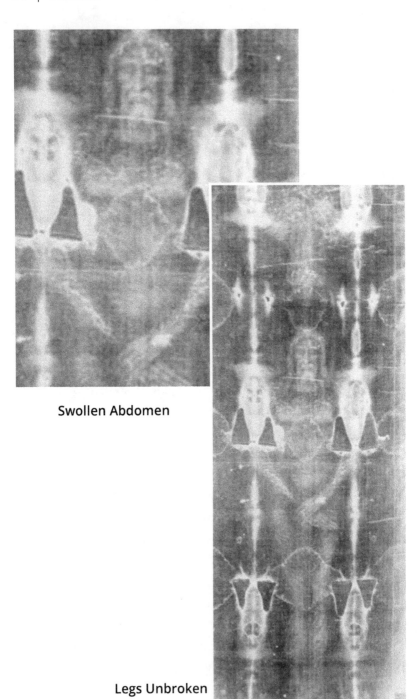

Swollen Abdomen

Legs Unbroken

6) Psalms 34:20 "He keepeth all his bones: not one of them is broken." Once again, David prophesied a unique facet of the Messiah's death: no broken bones. In order to expedite or induce death the legs were broken so that the victim could no longer lock his knees in order to breathe. Although clearly crucified the man of the Shroud's legs are unbroken. John cites this exact event as follows:

> John 19:31–36 "It was the Day of Preparation, and the next day was a festival Shabbat. So that the bodies should not remain on the execution stake during Shabbat, the Judean leaders asked Pilate to have the legs broken and to have the bodies taken away. So the soldiers came and broke the legs of the first and then the other who had been executed with Yeshua. Now when they came to Yeshua and saw that He was already dead, they did not break His legs. But one of the soldiers pierced His side with a spear, and immediately blood and water came out. He who has seen it has testified, and his testimony is true. He knows that he is telling the truth, so that you also may believe. These things happened so that the Scripture would be fulfilled, "Not a bone of His shall be broken."" TLV

Once again, we shall settle on a conservative 1 in 10^4. Another prophecy of Zechariah is also fulfilled in the image on the Shroud.

> Zechariah 12:10 "And I will pour upon the house of David, and upon the inhabitants of Jerusalem, the spirit of grace and of supplications: and they shall look upon me whom they have pierced, and they shall mourn for him, as

one mourneth for *his* only *son*, and shall be in bitterness for him, as one that is in bitterness for *his* firstborn."

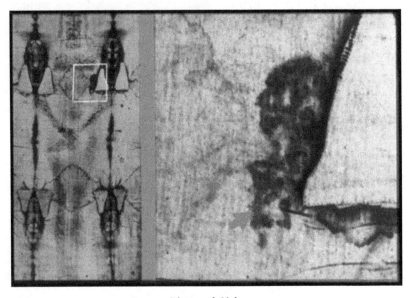

Pierced Side

Clearly visible between the fifth and sixth ribs is the normal "coup de grace" inflicted to ensure death. The size and shape of the wound matches the Roman "lancia: lance" which John's Gospel says was used. The placement and angle would pierce the pericardial sac. Due to the tremendous scourging which is visible on the Shroud there would be a build-up of the bloody fluid in the chest cavity. As blood and serum do not separate in the body until after death, the "blood and water" seen by John are a confirmation that Yeshua was already dead. Clearly there is evidence for both blood and serous fluid flowing from the wound in the side. Since it was traditional for a Roman soldier to use this tactic to ensure or confirm death we will lower our figure to 1×10^2.

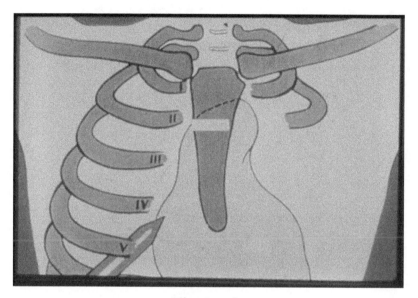

Ribs, Lancia

So the result is that there are seven specifically Messianic prophecies fulfilled in the image on the Shroud and with a cumulative probability of using Stoner's methodology 2.8×10^{26}. Then even if we add an extra 12 billion people to Stoner's original projection we arrive at a probability figure of 1×10^{16}. That would be the probability that any other man's death and burial would fulfill the same prophecies and mirror the passion of Yeshua.

Perhaps one more thing to consider is something seen on the Shroud that is not specifically prophesied but surely implied in prophecy: the Crown of Thorns and its connection to the rejection of the "Kingship" of Yeshua and the mocking of the Messiah of Israel over that rejection.

When the people demanded of Hashem a "king" like the other nations, Samuel was greatly grieved. It, in my opinion, serves as a type and shadow of the rejection of Messiah to come.

> 1Samuel 8:7 "Then Adonai said to Samuel, "Listen to the voice of the people in all that they say to you. For they have not rejected you, rather they have rejected Me from being king over them." TLV

David prophesies it in the same Psalm that so clearly presages the crucifixion.

> Psalms 22:7–9 "Am I a worm, and not a man? Am I a scorn of men, despised by people? All who see me mock me. They curl their lips, shaking their heads: Rely on Adonai! Let Him deliver him! Let Him rescue him—since he delights in Him!" TLV

Even Isaiah declares that the one despised will be the chosen one to whom kings and princes will bow.

> Isaiah 49:7 "Thus says Adonai, the Redeemer of Israel, their Holy One, to the One despised, to the One the nation abhors, to a servant of rulers: "Kings will see and arise, princes will also bow down, because of Adonai who is faithful, the Holy One of Israel who has chosen you."" TLV

While I will not assign a probability here, the rejection of the Kingship of Messiah is clearly connected to the Crown of Thorns. Three of the four Gospels mention it and each time it is in the context of a mocking rejection of Yeshua as King.

> John 19:2–3 "The soldiers twisted together a crown of thorns and put it on His head, and dressed Him in a

purple robe. They kept coming up to Him, saying, "Hail, the King of the Jews!" and slapping Him over and over."

John 19:14–16 "It was the Day of Preparation for Passover, about the sixth hour. And Pilate said to the Judean leaders, "Behold, your king!" They shouted back, "Take Him away! Take Him away! Execute Him!" Pilate said to them, "Should I execute your king?" The ruling kohanim answered, "We have no king but Caesar!" Finally, Pilate handed Yeshua over to be crucified." TLV

Matthew 27:28–31 "And they stripped him, and put on him a scarlet robe. And when they had platted a crown of thorns, they put *it* upon his head, and a reed in his right hand; and they bowed the knee before him, and mocked him, saying, Hail, King of the Jews! And they spit upon him, and took the reed, and smote him on the head. And after that they had mocked him, they took the robe off from him, and put his own raiment on him, and led him away to crucify *him*."

Matthew 27:39–43 "And they that passed by reviled him, wagging their heads, and saying, Thou that destroyest the temple, and buildest *it* in three days, save thyself. If thou be the Son of God, come down from the cross. Likewise also the chief priests mocking *him*, with the scribes and elders, said, He saved others; himself he cannot save. If he be the King of Israel, let him now come down from the cross, and we will believe him. He trusted in God; let him deliver him now, if he will have him: for he said, I am the Son of God."

Mark 15:17–20 "And they clothed him with purple, and platted a crown of thorns, and put it about his *head*, and began to salute him, Hail, King of the Jews! And they smote him on the head with a reed, and did spit upon him, and bowing *their* knees worshipped him. And when they had mocked him, they took off the purple from him, and put his own clothes on him, and led him out to crucify him."

Since the Crown of Thorns connected with a victim of crucifixion is virtually singular to the person of Yeshua, it is only logical that it strengthens greatly the probability that this burial garment briefly held his body. It also follows that it strengthens the case for authenticity as well as the case for prophetic fulfillment.

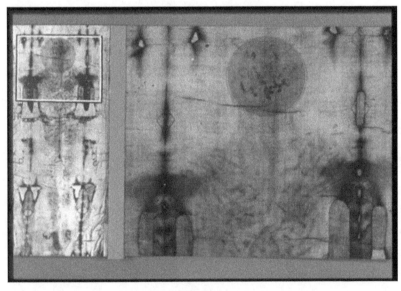

Crown of Thorns

Amos 3:7 "Surely the Lord GOD will do *nothing,* but he revealeth his secret unto his servants the prophets." (Emphasis added)

One of the key principles of Biblical Hermeneutics is prophetic fulfillment. The case for authenticity can only be strengthened by the incredible amount of fulfillment we've seen. Yeshua, when asked for a sign, made reference to the Book of Jonah making a prophetic connection to His death, burial and resurrection. We shall examine that next.

THE SIGN OF THE PROPHET JONAH

Matthew 12:38-40 "Then certain of the scribes and of the Pharisees answered, saying, Master, we would see a sign from thee. But he answered and said unto them, An evil and adulterous generation seeketh after a sign; and there shall no sign be given to it, but the sign of the prophet Jonas: For as Jonas was three days and three nights in the whale's belly; so shall the Son of man be three days and three nights in the heart of the earth."

Twice in the Gospel of Matthew, and again in the Gospel of Luke, Yeshua says the sign of the prophet Jonas (Jonah) is the only sign to be given. In the first instance the scribes and Pharisees ask for a sign. In Matthew 16 the Pharisees and Sadducees come together with the same request.

Matthew 16:1–4 "The Pharisees also with the Sadducees came, and tempting desired him that he would shew them a sign from heaven. He answered and said unto them, When it is evening, ye say, *It will be* fair weather: for the sky is red and lowering, O *ye* hypocrites, ye can discern the face of the sky; but can ye not *discern* the signs of the times? A wicked and adulterous generation seeketh after a sign; and there shall no sign be given unto it, but the sign of the prophet Jonas. And he left them, and departed."

Finally in the Gospel of Luke, Yeshua simply tells the pressing crowd the same thing.

Luke 11:29–30 "And when the people were gathered thick together, he began to say, This is an evil generation: they seek a sign; and there shall no sign be given it, but the sign of Jonas the prophet. For as Jonas was a sign unto the Ninevites, so shall also the Son of man be to this generation."

Surprisingly, the Haf Torah portion read on Yom Kippur, the Feast of Atonement, is the entire book of Jonah. Surely the significance that a believer in Yeshua would immediately notice is the clear connection between the death, burial and resurrection of Yeshua to Jonah's sojourn and release from the belly of the great fish. However, rabbinical sources take a different tack. Chabad.org presents the following: "Two primary reasons are given for reading the Book of Jonah as the *haftorah* of the Yom Kippur afternoon services: a) The story of Jonah teaches us how no one is beyond the reach of G-d's hand. Just as Jonah's endeavor to escape G-d's providence was unsuccessful, so, too, we are incapable of eluding divine justice for transgressions we may have committed, b) on a more uplifting note: G-d spared the people of Nineveh although He had already decreed that they would be destroyed because of their evil ways. This teaches us that no matter our past behavior, G-d's benevolence and mercy awaits us if we only repent full-heartedly." [The text goes on to refer to an article which considers Jonah to be an allegory of everyone's life.] "The Book of Jonah, read in its entirety during the Yom Kippur afternoon services, is the story of your life. This is what the Kabbalah says: You are Jonah. The *real* you, for "Jonah"—in Kabbalistic parlance—is another name for the soul. Hence, the story of Jonah is the story of a soul's journey here on earth. Thus, on Yom Kippur, as we examine our lives and consider our purpose in this world, we remember the historical Jonah whose real-life narrative symbolizes our spiritual odyssey."[9]

Though Yeshua states specifically to the scribes and Pharisees that he would lie in the earth for a mere three days and nights before being restored, neither the allegory, nor the traditional teaching make any mention of the implication of Scripture that Jonah died in the belly of the fish and was restored by the *chesed* of G-d.

> Jonah 2:1–6 "Then Jonah prayed unto the LORD his God out of the fish's belly, And said, I cried by reason of mine affliction unto the LORD, and he heard me; out of the belly of hell cried I, *and* thou heardest my voice. For thou hadst cast me into the deep, in the midst of the seas; and the floods compassed me about; all thy billows and

---

9   Chabad.Org: http://www.chabad.org/holidays/JewishNewYear/template_cdo/aid/568512/jewish/Why-do-we-read-the-Book-of-Jonah-onYom-Kippur.htm
& http://www.chabad.org/holidays/JewishNewYear/template_cdo/aid/430304/jewish/The-Story-of-Your-Life.htm

thy waves passed over me. Then I said, I am cast out of thy sight; yet I will look again toward thy holy temple. The waters compassed me about, *even* to the soul: the depth closed me round about, the weeds were wrapped bout my head. I went down to the bottoms of the mountains; the earth with her bars *was* about me forever; yet hast thou brought up my life from corruption, O LORD my God. When my soul fainted within me I remembered the LORD: and my prayer came in unto thee, into thine holy temple."

In verse two Jonah said he cries out to G-D from the very "belly" of "hell." Let us examine the words in Hebrew: sh°ôl; she'ôl, שאול שְׁאֹל «ôl; sheh-ole´ "From H7592; hades or the world of the dead (as if subterranean retreat), including its accessories and inmates: grave, hell, pit."

Furthermore, in verse six Jonah declares that G-D "brought up." 'âlâh, עלה; aw-law´ "A primitive root; to *ascend*, intransitively (*be high*) or active (*mount*); used in a great variety of senses, primary and secondary, literally and figuratively: arise (up), (cause to, make to) come (up), cut off, dawn, depart, exalt, excel, fall, fetch up, get up, (make to) go (away, up), grow (over), increase, lay, leap, levy, lift (self) up, light, [make] up, X mention, mount up, offer, make to pay, + perfect, prefer, put (on), ___**raise,**___ ___**recover, restore**___, (make to) rise (up), scale, set (up), shoot forth (up), (begin to) sprint (up), stir up, take away (up), work." (Emphasis added)

"...my life;" חי_chay; *khah'ee* "From H2421; *alive*; hence *raw* (flesh); *fresh*..."

"...from corruption;" shachath, שתיחות; *shakh'-ath* "From H7743; a *pit* (especially as a trap); figuratively *destruction*: corruption, destruction, ditch, grave, pit."

But what, you might ask, is the connection between Jonah, Yeshua, and the Shroud of Turin? It is the absence of any sign of corruption in spite of the specific evidence of death. Furthermore, it is the fulfillment of the prophetic words of David as cited by both Peter and Paul concerning these very things. David, in Psalms 68 speaks of Yeshua's victory over death, hell and the grave in this fashion:

> Psalms 68:18–20 "Thou has ascended on high, thou hast led captivity captive: thou hast received gifts for men; yea, *for* the rebellious also, that the LORD God might dwell *among them.* Blessed *be* the Lord, *who* daily loadeth us *with benefits, even* the God of our salvation. Selah. *He that is* our God *is* the God of salvation; and unto GOD the Lord *belong* the issues from death."

The Apostle Paul specifies to the church at Ephesus that this very Scripture was prophetically fulfilled in Christ.

> Ephesians 4:8–10 "Wherefore he saith, When he ascended up on high, he led captivity captive, and gave gifts unto men. (Now that he ascended, what is it but that he also descended first unto the lower parts of the earth? He that descended is the same also that ascended up far above all heavens, that he might fill all things.)"

Furthermore, David again prophetically declares that the Messiah would not see corruption and that very text is referenced by both Peter and Paul:

Psalms 16:10 "For thou wilt not leave my soul in hell; neither wilt thou suffer thine Holy One to see corruption. Thou wilt shew me the path of life: in thy presence *is* fullness of joy; at thy right hand *there are* pleasures for evermore."

On the day of Pentecost, Peter tells the crowd that has gathered:

Acts 2:22–37 "Men of Israel, hear these words! Yeshua he-Natzrati—a Man authenticated to you by God with mighty deeds and wonders and signs God performed through Him in your midst, as you yourselves know this Yeshua, given over by God's predetermined plan and foreknowledge, nailed to the cross by the hand of lawless men, you killed. But God raised Him up, releasing Him from the pains of death, since it was impossible for Him to be held by it. For David says about Him, 'I saw Adonai always before me, for He is at my right hand so that I might not be shaken. Therefore my heart was glad and my tongue rejoiced; moreover, my body also will live in hope, because You will not abandon my soul to Sheol or let Your Holy One see decay. You have made known to me the paths of life; You will fill me with joy in Your presence.' Brothers, I can confidently tell you that patriarch David died and was buried—his tomb is with us to this day. So because he was a prophet and knew God had sworn with an oath to him to seat one of his descendants on his throne, David saw beforehand and spoke of Messiah's resurrection—that He was not abandoned to Sheol, and His body did not see decay. This Yeshua God raised up—we all are witnesses! Therefore, being exalted to the right hand of God and receiving from the Father the promise of the Ruach ha-Kodesh, He poured out this—what you now see and hear. For David did not ascend into the heavens; yet he himself says, 'Adonai said to my Lord, "Sit at my right hand, until I make Your enemies a footstool for Your feet.' Therefore, let the whole house of Israel know for certain that God has made Him—this Yeshua whom you had crucified—both Lord and Messiah! Now when they heard this, they were cut to the heart and said to Peter and the rest of the emissaries, 'Fellow brethren, what shall we do?'" TLV

Later, in the Book of Acts, Paul makes the same case:

Acts 13:26–39 "Brothers, sons of the family of Abraham and those among you who are God-fearers, it is to us the message of this salvation has been sent. For those who live in Jerusalem and their rulers—not recognizing Him or the sayings of the Prophets that are read every Shabbat—fulfilled these words by condemning Him. Though they found no charge worthy of a death sentence, they asked Pilate to have Him executed. When they had carried out all that had been written about Him, they took Him down from the tree and laid Him in a tomb. But God raised Him from the dead! For many days He appeared to those who had come up from the Galilee to Jerusalem, who are now His witnesses to the people. And we proclaim to you Good News—the promise to the fathers has arrived! For God has fulfilled this promise to the children—to us—by raising up Yeshua, as it is also written in the second psalm: 'You are My Son. Today I have become Your Father.' But since He raised Him up from the dead, never to return to decay, He has spoken in this way, 'I will give you the holy and sure mercies of David.' Therefore He also says in another psalm, 'You will not permit Your Holy One to see decay.' For after David had served God's purpose in his own generation, he went to sleep and was laid with his fathers and saw decay. But the One whom God raised up did not see decay. Therefore, let it be known to you, brothers that through this One is proclaimed to you the removal of sins, including all those from which you could not be set right by the Torah of Moses. Through this One everyone who keeps trusting is made righteous." TLV

Note that when Peter finished his sermon, three thousand souls were saved and in the case of Paul, the entire city showed up the following week to hear more!

Acts 2:41–42 "So those who received his message were immersed, and that day about three thousand souls were added. They were devoting themselves to the teaching of the emissaries and to fellowship, to breaking bread and to prayers." TLV

Acts 13:42–44 "As Paul and Barnabas were going out, the people kept begging them to speak these things to them the next Shabbat. When the synagogue meeting broke up, many of the Jewish people and God-fearing inquirers followed Paul and Barnabas, who were speaking with them and trying to persuade them to continue in the grace of God. The following Shabbat, almost the entire city came together to hear the word of the Lord." TLV

During my first pilgrimage to Israel, I visited the traditional site of the Upper Room where Yeshua celebrated Passover before His passion and death, and also where the Holy Spirit fell on the disciples who were waiting for the promise. I discovered to my great surprise that the Tomb of David still rests directly below that same Upper Room! Suddenly, the literal reality of the second chapter of the book of Acts became crystal clear. Those who made a pilgrimage to the Tomb of David from many nations on that Pentecost feast day, could clearly hear the worship of the disciples from the open portico above. Peter then could literally point to David's sepulcher for all to see.

It is also interesting to note that Yeshua told the religious leaders that "a" wicked and perverse generation would seek a sign, leaving, in my opinion, room for a future fulfillment. Yet to the pressing crowd he specifically said "this" wicked and perverse generation.

On the Shroud of Turin therefore, we see an image...An image of the atoning sacrificial Lamb of G-D whose body saw death and yet not corruption. The image allows us to see up close and personal: the nail-scarred hands, the brutally scourged body, the pierced side and the marred face. As Isaiah prophesied, we can "consider" (perceive and understand) what we had never heard before. We can "see" (behold and discern; even stare at) what we had never been told! How is it then that His Chosen People, the precious people of Israel still do not see? According to the Apostle Paul it is only a temporary thing:

> Romans 11:25–27 "For I would not, brethren, that ye should be ignorant of this mystery, lest ye should be wise in your own conceits; that blindness in part is happened to Israel, until the fullness of the Gentiles be come in. And so

all Israel shall be saved: as it is written, There shall come out of Sion the Deliverer, and shall turn away ungodliness from Jacob: For this is my covenant unto them, when I shall take away their sins."

As a child would ask during a long trip, I must also ask, "Are we there yet?!" Have we not reached the point in this world where the *time of the Gentiles* is fulfilled?

Luke 21:24 "And they shall fall by the edge of the sword, and shall be led away captive into all nations: and Jerusalem shall be trodden down of the Gentiles, until the times of the Gentiles be fulfilled."

In June of 1967, the tiny fledgling nation of Israel, born again in 1948 from the ashes of WWII, was attacked by five of its Arab neighbors, who were in turn supported by the P.L.O. (Palestine Liberation Organization) and an additional eight Arab nations. When the *Six Day War*, as it came to be known, was over, Israel once again controlled the "Old City" of Jerusalem for the first time since 70 AD. Even the surprise attack of the Yom Kippur War of 1973 did not cause them to lose that territory. Jerusalem, after nearly two thousand years was no longer "trodden down of the Gentiles."

Yeshua and Paul both refer to the end point of the "time of the Gentiles." Yeshua connects it to the return of the Jews to the Promised Land and to Jerusalem itself. Isaiah the prophet foretold of the restoration of the nation of Israel in its homeland and specifically in Jerusalem:

Isaiah 66:8 "Who hath heard such a thing? Who hath seen such things: Shall the earth be made to bring forth in one day? *or* shall a nation be born at once? For as soon as Zion travailed, she brought forth her children..."

Isaiah 66:13 "As one whom his mother comforteth, so will I comfort you; and ye shall be comforted in Jerusalem."

Furthermore, Paul declares that at the same time Israel would be saved according to the covenant that G-D had promised through the prophet Jeremiah:

Jeremiah 31:30–34 "But every one shall die for his iniquity: every man that eateth the sour grape, his teeth shall be set on edge. Behold, the days come, saith the LORD, that I will make a new covenant with the house of Israel, and with the house of Judah: Not according to the covenant that I made with their fathers in the day *that* I took them by the hand to bring them out of the land of Egypt; which my covenant they brake, although I was an husband unto them, saith the LORD: But this *shall be* the covenant that I will make with the house of Israel; After those days, saith the LORD, I will put my law in their inward parts, and write it in their hearts; and will be their God, they shall be my people. And they shall teach no more every man his neighbor, and every man his brother, saying, Know the LORD: for they shall all know me, from the least of them unto the greatest of them, saith the LORD: for I will forgive their iniquity, and I will remember their sin no more."

A "new covenant" which Yeshua boldly proclaimed to His disciples as they celebrated the Passover that would end with His passion, Death, and ultimately Resurrection.

> Matthew 26:28 "For this is My blood of the new covenant, which is poured out for many for the removal of sins."

The same "new covenant" Paul describes in great detail throughout the book of Hebrews as the very fulfillment of G-d's promise:

> Hebrews 8:6–12 "But now Yeshua has obtained a more excellent ministry, insofar as He is the mediator of a better covenant which has been enacted on better promises. For if that first one had been faultless, there would not have been discourse seeking a second. For finding fault with them, He says, 'Behold, days are coming, says Adonai, when I will inaugurate a new covenant with the house of Israel and with the house of Judah. It will not be like the covenant I made with their fathers on the day when I took them by the hand to lead them out of the land of Egypt. For they did not remain in My covenant, and I did not care for them, says Adonai. For this is the covenant that I will make with the house of Israel after those days, says Adonai. I will put My Torah into their mind, and upon their hearts I will write it. And I will be their God, and they shall be My people. And no more will they teach, each one his fellow citizen and each one his brother, saying, 'Know Adonai,' because all will know Me, from the least of them to the greatest. For I will be merciful toward their iniquities, and their sins I will remember no more.'" TLV

This covenant is clearly connected to the "*blood of sprinkling.*"

> Hebrews 12:24 "...and to Yeshua, the Mediator of a new covenant, and to the sprinkled blood that speaks of something better than the blood of Abel."

The Apostle Paul, who authors 60% of the New Testament, consistently offers evidence that Yeshua is indeed Messiah, and often provides connections that line up with the Shroud of Turin. Who is this man Paul, who by his own admission, attempted to destroy the ekklesia?

> Galatians 1:13–14 "For you have heard of my earlier behavior in Judaism—how I persecuted God's community beyond measure and tried to destroy it. I was even advancing within Judaism behond many my own age among my people, being a more extreme observer of my fathers' traditions." TLV

In our next chapter, we will examine Paul's origin and transformation.

A RABBI NAMED SAUL

Acts 9:1–2 "And Saul, yet breathing out threatenings and slaughter against the disciples of the Lord, went unto the high priest, and desired of him letters to Damascus to the synagogues, that if he found any of this way, whether they were men or women, he might bring them bound unto Jerusalem."

Acts 22:3–5 "I am verily a man *which am* a Jew, born in Tarsus, *a city* in Cilicia, yet brought up in this city at the feet of Gamaliel, *and* taught according to the perfect manner of the law of the fathers, and was zealous toward God, as ye all are this day. And I persecuted this way unto the death, binding and delivering into prisons both men and women. As also the high priest doth bear me witness, and all the estate of the elders: from whom also I received letters unto

> the brethren, and went to Damascus, to bring them which
> were there bound unto Jerusalem, for to be punished."

Years ago, on my very first pilgrimage to Israel, I had a
discussion with an Orthodox Rabbi concerning Saul.
It seems that he had always been taught that Saul was a
Sadducee, and he asked why I had stated with such certainty that
Saul was in fact a Pharisee. When I mentioned that Saul was a
student of Gamaliel, he became incredulous that I should even
know the name. "You *know* Gamaliel?" he cried. I shared with him
several Scriptures found in the Book of Acts. The Rabbi certainly
knew that Gamaliel was a Pharisee and that called into question
what he had clearly been taught concerning Saul. To underscore
that issue, perhaps the one Scripture most germane to this study
is the following:

> Acts 23:6–8 "But when Paul perceived that the one
> part were Sadducees, and the other Pharisees, he cried out
> in the council, Men *and* brethren, I am a Pharisee, the sons
> of a Pharisee: of the hope and resurrection of the dead I am
> called in question. And when he had so said, there arose
> a dissension between the Pharisees and the Sadducees:
> and the multitude was divided. For the Sadducees say that
> there is no resurrection, neither angel, nor spirit: but the
> Pharisees confess both."

Saul, once a vicious persecutor of the sect now known as
the Nazarenes, has been transformed into "Tzuar" the strongest
defender of the faith who would go on to author sixty percent of
the New Testament. His story of the Damascus Road experience
is told twice in all of his writings. Furthermore, his conviction of

the Resurrection of Yeshua is the focal point of numerous passages along with intriguing hints that can easily be seen to point to the Shroud and its mysterious image.

In the Book of Acts, Paul uses the promise of resurrection so effectively that he nearly brings salvation to King Agrippa.

> Acts 26:1–8 "Then Agrippa said unto Paul, Thou art permitted to speak for thyself. Then Paul stretched forth the hand, and answered for himself: I think myself happy, king Agrippa, because I shall answer for myself this day before thee touching all the things whereof I am accused of the Jews: Especially *because I know* thee to be expert in all customs and questions which are among the Jews: wherefore I beseech thee to hear me patiently. My manner of life from my youth, which was at the first among mine own nation at Jerusalem, know all the Jews; which knew me from the beginning, if they would testify, that after the most straitest sect of our religion I lived a Pharisee. Now I stand and am judged for the hope of the promise made of God unto our fathers: Unto which *promise* our twelve tribes, instantly serving *God* day and night, hope to come. For which hope's sake, king Agrippa, I am accused of the Jews. Why should it be thought a thing incredible with you, that God should raise the dead?"

> Acts 26:21–23 "For this reason some Judeans seized me in the Temple and tried to put me to death. Since I have had God's help, to this day I have stood here testifying to both small and great. I am saying nothing but what the Prophets and Moses said was going to happen—that the Messiah was to suffer and that, being first to rise from the

dead, He would proclaim light both to our people and to the nations." TLV

Acts 26:26–28 "_For the king knoweth of these things,_ _before whom also I speak freely; for I am persuaded that none of_ _these things are hidden from him; for this thing was not done in_ _a corner._ King Agrippa, believest thou the prophets? I know that thou believest. Then Agrippa said unto Paul, Almost thou persuadest me to be a Christian." (Emphasis added)

It was this very Scripture that raised for me the issue of a potential future fulfillment of Isaiah 52:13–15. Paul here asserts that *these* kings (Festus and Agrippa) already knew. Paul, by his own admission a strict Pharisee, declares that both Moses and the Prophets foretold the suffering, death, and resurrection of the Messiah, as well as the fact that he would be a light to both Jew and Gentile.

Writing to the church at Rome, the Apostle Paul also makes direct reference to the Isaiah passage in context and thereby confirms its connection to the salvation of the Jewish people.

Romans 10:15–16 "And how shall they preach, except they be sent? as it is written, How beautiful are the feet of them that preach the gospel of peace, and bring glad tidings of good things! But they have not all obeyed the gospel. For Esaias saith, Lord, who hath believed our report?"

In context, this quote of the Apostle Paul goes from Isaiah 52:7 to Isaiah 53:1, and therefore given that there were no chapter divisions as we know them, it automatically covers Isaiah 52:13–

15 which *IS* the report to which Paul refers. Nor does Paul stop at that juncture, but goes on to add:

> Romans 10:19–21 "But I say, Did not Israel know? First Moses saith, I will provoke you to jealousy by *them that are* no people, *and* by a foolish nation I will anger you. But Esaias is very bold, and saith, I was found of them that sought me not; I was made manifest unto them that asked not after me. But to Israel he saith, All day long I have stretched forth my hands unto a disobedient and gainsaying people."

Paul first cites Moishe from Deuteronomy 32:21

> Deuteronomy 32:20–21 "*And he said, I will hide my face from them,** I will see what their end *shall be*: for they *are* a very forward generation, children in whom *is* no faith. They have moved me to jealousy with *that which is* not God; they have provoked me to anger with their vanities: and I will move them to jealousy with *those which are* not a people; I will provoke them to anger with a foolish nation."

> (*More on the hidden face later.)

He then quotes Isaiah as found in several passages: Isaiah 49:6; **52:15**; 55:4–5; and 65:1–2 to confirm the *manifestation* of God's Messiah, even to the Gentiles.

> Isaiah 49:6 "And he said, It is a light thing that thou shouldest be my servant to raise up the tribes of Jacob, and to restore the preserved of Israel: I will also give thee for a

light to the Gentiles, that thou mayest be my salvation unto the end of the earth."

Isaiah 55:4–5 "Behold, I have given him *for* a witness to the people, a leader and commander to the people. Behold, thou shalt call a nation *that* thou knowest not, and nations *that* knew not thee shall run unto thee because of the LORD thy God, and for the Holy One of Israel;, for he hath glorified thee."

Isaiah 65:1–2 "I am sought of *them that* ask not *for me*; I am found of *them that* sought me not: I said, behold me, behold me, unto a nation *that* was not called by my name. I have spread out my hands all the day unto a rebellious people, which walketh in a way *that was* not good, after their own thoughts;"

Isaiah 52:15 *"So shall he sprinkle many nations; the kings shall shut their mouths at him: for that which had not been told them shall they see; and that which they had not heard shall they consider."* (Emphasis added)

The Hebrew word for "sprinkle" has a very unique and powerful significance that we will discuss throughout this work. Nâzâh, *naw-zaw'* נָזָה A primitive root; to *spirt*, that is, *besprinkle* (especially in expiation): sprinkle. BDB Definition: 1) to spurt, spatter, sprinkle 1a) (Qal) to spurt, spatter 1b) (Hiphil) to cause to spurt, sprinkle upon 2) to spring, leap 2a) (Hiphil) to cause to leap, startle.

The confirmation, once again, in the pivotal Isaiah 52:13–15 passage, is pointing out that a marred face and body would be seen and considered by those who had never heard before. The result would be the sprinkling and startling of nations (Gentiles) and even kings would be dumbfounded.

Continuing on in the context of the Book of Romans, Paul next declares that only a remnant of the seed of Abraham had received the report of the Isaiah prophecy. However, that in and of itself was a part of the plan of G-D in order that salvation might be extended to the nations.

> Romans 11:7–15 'What then? Israel hath not obtained that which he seeketh for, but the election hath obtained it, and the rest were blinded (According as it is written, God hath given them the spirit of slumber, eyes that they should not see, and ears that they should not hear;) unto this day And David saith, Let their table be made a snare, and a trap, and a stumbling block, and a recompense unto them" Let their eyes be darkened, that they may not see, and bow down their back always. I say then, Have they stumbled that they should fall? God forbid: but *rather* through their fall salvation *is come* unto the Gentiles, for to provoke them to jealousy. Now if the fall of them *be* riches of the world, and the diminishing of them the riches of the Gentiles; how much more their fullness? For I speak to you Gentiles, inasmuch as I am the apostle of the Gentiles, I magnify mine office: If by any means I may provoke to emulation *them which are* my flesh, and might save some of them. For if the casting away of them *be* the reconciling of the world, what *shall* the receiving *of them be*, but life from the dead?"

As we shall see, Paul explains even the very reason why the death of the Messiah would become a stumbling block to the Chosen People. Paul, later in the book of Hebrews, refers specifically to the "blood of sprinkling."

> Hebrews 12:24 "And to Yeshua, the Mediator of a new covenant, and to the sprinkled blood that speaks of something better than the blood of Abel." TLV

> Hebrews 9:11–15 "But when Messiah appeared as Kohen Gadol of the good things that have now come, passing through the greater and more perfect Tent not made with hands (that is to say not of this creation), He entered into the Holies once for all—not by the blood of goats and calves but by His own blood, having obtained eternal redemption. For if the blood of goats and bulls and the ashes of a heifer sprinkling those who have defiled sanctify for the cleansing of the flesh, how much more will the blood of Messiah— who through the eternal Spirit offered Himself without blemish to God—cleanse our conscience from dead works to serve the living God? For this reason He is the mediator of a new covenant, in order that those called may receive the promised eternal inheritance—since a death has taken place that redeems them from violations under the first covenant." TLV

Therefore, if we are to see and be startled and sprinkled by the blood, marred face and body of Mashiach, why would anyone be surprised that a "picture" would exist somewhere? Especially one that has throughout its history been known as "*acheiropoieton*" meaning *not made by human hands*; an image often copied but never duplicated; an image that has spanned the globe.

Even as this book reaches completion, that same mysterious image on the Shroud of Turin is being featured in a major motion picture following the story of a Roman soldier's search for the resurrected body of Yeshua. I was amazed to receive a call about the film from a fellow whose home church hosted my presentation this past November, 2015.[10]

Paul also, in his letter to the church at Corinth, points out that the resurrection is indeed the central message of the Gospel (good news).

The Resurrection of the Dead

1Corinthians 15:3–23 "For I also passed on to you first of all what I also received—that Messiah died for our sins according to the Scriptures, that He was buried, that He was raised on the third day according to the Scriptures, and that He appeared to Kefa, then to the Twelve. Then He appeared to over five hundred brothers and sisters at one time—most of them are still alive, though some have died. Then He appeared to Jacob, then to all the emissaries, and last of all, as to one untimely born, He also appeared to me. For I am the least of the emissaries, unworthy to be called an emissary because I persecuted God's community. But by the grace of God I am what I am. His grace toward me was not in vain. No, I worked harder than them all—yet not I, but the grace of God that was with me. Whether then it is I or they, so we proclaim, and so you believed. Now if Messiah is proclaimed—that He has been raised from the dead— how can some among you say that there is no resurrection of the dead? But if there is no resurrection of

10   Kevin Reynolds & Paul Aiello, **Risen**, (Sony Pictures, 2016)

the dead, not even Messiah has been raised! And if Messiah has not been raised, then our proclaiming is meaningless and your faith also is meaningless. Moreover, we are found to be false witnesses of God, because we testified about God that He raised up Messiah—whom He did not raise up, if in fact the dead are not raised. For if the dead are not raised, not even Messiah has been raised. And if Messiah has not been raised, our faith is futile—you are still in your sins. Then those also who have fallen asleep in Messiah have perished. If we have hoped in Messiah in this life alone, we are to be pitied more than all people. But now Messiah has been raised from the dead, the firstfruits of those who have fallen asleep. For since death came through a man, the resurrection of the dead also has come through a Man. For as in Adam all die, so also in Messiah will all be made alive. But each in its own order: Messiah the firstfruits; then, at His coming, those who belong to Messiah;" TLV

Paul, who had witnessed the martyrdom of Stephen, and who had persecuted both men and women to the death had become not only the leading missionary for the church, but also its leading apologist. Of course, the major issue in all of this is why the Messiah would die on a cross, when the Torah says that such a death is a curse. Once again, the issue is dealt with specifically by Paul, to the churches at both Corinth and Galatia.

1Corinthians 1:17–25 "For Messiah sent me not to immerse, but to proclaim the Good News—not with cleverness of speech, so that the cross of Messiah would not be made of no effect. For the message of the cross is foolishness to those who are perishing, but to us who are being saved it is the power of God. For it is written, "I will destroy the wisdom of the wise and bring to nothing the understanding of the intelligent (Isaiah 29:14). Where is the wise one? Where is the Torah scholar? Where is the debater of this age? Hasn't God made foolish the wisdom of the world? For seeing that—in God's wisdom—the world through its wisdom did not know God, God was pleased— through the foolishness of the message proclaimed—to save those who believe. For Jewish people ask for signs and Greek people seek after wisdom, *but we proclaim Messiah crucified—a stumbling block to Jewish people and foolishness to Gentile people*, but to those who are called (both Jewish and Greek people), Messiah, the power of God and the wisdom of God. For the foolishness of God is wiser than men, and the weakness of God is stronger than men." TLV (Emphasis added)

Why would Hashem send the Messiah, first of all to die, but furthermore to be accursed by dying on a cross, knowing that such a death would create a stumbling block to the Jews and seem utterly foolish to the Gentiles? The prophet Isaiah gives us one clear statement about the thoughts of the Most High.

Isaiah 55:8–9 "For my thoughts *are* not your thoughts, neither *are* your ways, saith the LORD. For *as* the heavens are higher than the earth, so are my ways higher than your ways, and my thoughts than your thoughts."

But Paul offers a compelling understanding to the church at Galatia.

Galatians 3:6–26 "Just as Abraham "believed God, and it was credited to him as righteousness," know then that those who have faith are children of Abraham. The Scriptures, foreseeing that God would justify the Gentiles by faith, proclaimed the Good News to Abraham in advance, saying, "All nations shall be blessed through you." So then, the faithful are blessed along with Abraham, the faithful one. For all who rely on the deeds of Torah are under a curse— for the Scriptures say, "Cursed is everyone who does not keep doing everything written in the scroll of the Torah." It is clear that no one is set right before God by Torah, for "the righteous shall live by emunah." However, Torah is not based on trust and faithfulness; on the contrary, "the one who does these things shall live by them." Messiah liberated us from Torah's curse, having become a curse for us (for it is written, "Cursed is everyone who hangs on a tree")—in order that through Messiah Yeshua the blessing of Abraham might come to the Gentiles, so we might receive the promise of the Ruach through trusting faith. Brothers and sisters, I speak in human terms: even with a man's covenant, once it has been confirmed, no one cancels it or adds to it. Now the promises were spoken to Abraham and to his seed. It doesn't say, "and to seeds," as of man, but as of one, "and to your seed," who is the Messiah. What I am saying is this: Torah, which came 430 years later, does not cancel the covenant previously confirmed by God, so as to make the promise ineffective. For if the inheritance is based on law, it is no longer based on a promise But God has graciously given it to Abraham by means of a promise Then why the Torah? It was added because of wrongdoings until the Seed would come—to whom the promise had been made. It was arranged through angels by the hand of an intermediary. Now an intermediary is not for one party alone—but God is one. Then is the Torah against the promises of God? May it never be! For if a law had been given that could impart life, certainly righteousness would have been based on law. But the Scripture has locked up the whole world under sin, so that the promise based on trust in Messiah Yeshua might be given to those who trust. Now before faith came, we were being guarded under Torah—bound together until the coming faith would be revealed. Therefore the Torah became our guardian to lead us to Messiah, so that we might be made right based on trusting. But now that faith has come, we are no longer under a guardian. For you are all sons of God through trusting in Messiah Yeshua." TLV

In context, moreover, that entire passage begins with this incredible statement from Paul.

Galatians 3:1 "O foolish Galatians, who cast a spell on you? *Before your eyes* Yeshua the Messiah was *clearly portrayed* as crucified." TLV (Emphasis added)

In plain English this could be easily stated in front of your very eyes Yeshua was "engraved" (written) as crucified. Since it is believed that Paul likely established the ekklesia at Galatia sometime around 55–56 AD, what could they possible have *seen* that revealed the Messiah as crucified?

To sum up this facet of the story then as exactly as Yeshua declared to His disciples:

John 3:14–15 "And as Moses lifted up the serpent in the wilderness, even so must the Son of man be lifted up: that whosoever believeth in him should not perish, but have eternal life."

The serpent was a curse sent to a rebellious people and its bite was fatal. But when Moishe lifted a serpent on a pole for the people to see, they were healed of the poison of the serpent. (Numbers 21:5–9) We **ALL** are a sinful and rebellious people, who like Adam before us, have been "bitten" by the serpent: sinned and come short of HIS glory. (Romans 3:23) But Messiah Yeshua was lifted up on that cross so that we might live and live eternally.

Romans 6:23 "For sin's payment is death, but God's gracious gift is eternal life in Messiah Yeshua our Lord." TLV

Colossian 2:8–15 "See that no one takes you captive through philosophy and empty deception, according to the tradition of men and the basic principles of the world rather than Messiah. For all the fullness of Deity lives bodily in Him, and in Him you have been filled to fullness. He is the head over every ruler and authority. In Him you were also circumcised with a circumcision done not by hand, in the stripping away of the body of the flesh through the circumcision of Messiah. You were buried along with Him in immersion, through which you also were raised with Him by trusting in the working of God, who raised Him from the dead. When you were dead in your sins and the uncircumcision of your flesh, God made you alive together with Him when He pardoned us all our transgressions. He wiped out the handwritten record of debts with the decrees against us, which was hostile to us. He took it away by nailing it to the cross. After disarming the principalities and powers, He made a public spectacle of them, triumphing over them in the cross." TLV

Yet there are even more interesting quotes from Paul, which in my opinion, point to the Shroud. In his letter to the church at Corinth, after describing in depth that the best gift of the new church is the gift of agape love, Paul suddenly interjects a seemingly unrelated statement.

> 1 Corinthians 13:12 "For now we see through a glass, darkly; but then face to face: now I know in part; but then shall I know even as also I am know."

Glass: esoptron. Thayer Definition: 1) a mirror. Strong's: *es'-op-tron* From G1519 and a presumed derivative of G3700; a *mirror* (for *looking into*): -glass. Strong's: Darkly: ainigma, *ah'ee-nig-ma* from a derivative of G136 (in its primary sense); an *obscure* saying ("enigma"), that is, (abstractly) *obscureness*: - X darkly.

More plainly stated in modern English: "Now we see an obscure mirrored image, an enigma, *but then* we shall see *face to face*." (Which I will address further in the chapter "Face to Face.") If the statement is meant to be a direct comparison, then what obscure mirrored image could Paul have referred to that was also an enigma? Furthermore, it's an enigma that would only be resolved when we see Him "face to face." The only logical answer is the Shroud of Turin, which down through the centuries, would be known in numerous ways as "the miraculous image of the Savior."

Later on in his second letter to Corinth, another reference appears to "beholding a face in a mirror."

2 Corinthians 3:18 "But we all, with unveiled face beholding as in a mirror the glory of the Lord, are being transformed into the same image from glory to glory—just as from the Lord, who is the Spirit."

In context here, Paul connects this second "image" reference with removing the "veil" of blindness and the transformation of the viewer by the Ruach Ha Kodesh. During our trip to Turin to conduct the initial research, an investigative reporter from New York was among those assigned to cover the story. By his own admission he was an alcoholic and an abusive husband who thought the entire trip was a colossal waste of time. Sitting in the rear of St. John's Cathedral and gazing upon the face of the Shroud, he found himself convicted of his own sinfulness and became transformed by the love of Yeshua. He did not worship the "cloth" but instead like those who were healed by gazing at the serpent on the pole, he was delivered from sin and death.

Now we shall look at how such a "miraculous image" was known historically long before the first documented display of the Shroud of Turin. The image, which had many names down through the centuries, could actually resolve the missing years of the Shroud, and is also attested to by modern technology.

THE SHROUD IN ART:

ORIGINAL ACHEIROPOIETON?

Exodus 20:4–5 "Thou shalt not make unto thee any graven image, or any likeness *of anything* that *is* in heaven above, or that *is* in the earth beneath, or that *is* in the water under the earth: Thou shalt not bow down thyself to them, nor serve them: for I the LORD thy God *am* a jealous God, visiting the iniquity of the fathers upon the children unto the third and fourth *generation* of them that hate me;"

On the surface, the commandment of Exodus 20:4–5, repeated five more times throughout the Pentateuch, seems to mitigate against the potential authenticity of the Shroud of Turin. Unless of course it can be demonstrated beyond a shadow of a doubt that the image was not in any way, shape, or form created by the hand of man. Having had the awesome privilege of serving with STURP in the 1978 testing of the Shroud, and the more than three years of analyzing the data collected during those six twenty-four hour days, it is my considered opinion that the most significant finding of the team was the conclusion presented in October, 1981.

"We can conclude for now that the shroud image is that of a real human form of a scourged, crucified man. It is NOT the product of an artist. The bloodstains are composed of hemoglobin and also give a positive test for serum albumin. The image is an ongoing mystery and until further chemical studies are made, perhaps by this group of scientists, or perhaps by some scientists in the future, the problem remains unsolved."[11]

The Shroud is *not* the creation of a man, and the numerous unique qualities of its incredible image present an unsolved mystery as to *how* it was created. In the thirty-five year interim nothing has happened to change that conclusion: the Shroud is not the work of human hands, period. The only drawback would be that there is no unbroken tradition taking the cloth back to John's Gospel.

> John 20:4–9 "So they ran both together: and the other disciple did outrun Peter, and came first to the sepulcher. And he stooping down, *and looking in*, saw the linen clothes lying; yet went he not in. Then cometh Simon Peter following him, and went into the sepulcher, and seeth the linen clothes lie, And the napkin, that was about his head, not lying with the linen clothes, but wrapped together in a place by itself. Then went in also that other disciple, which came first to the sepulcher, and he saw, and believed.

---

11 **STURP Summary**

For as yet they knew not the scripture, that he must rise again from the dead."

The Scripture is clear that the disciples Peter and John found the burial linens in the tomb and that there were at least two pieces. But the Scripture also intimates that something about the burial garments convinces John of the resurrection even though he did not "understand or perceive that it was necessary/needful" for Yeshua to rise from the dead: εἴδω, eidō, i'-do A primary verb; used only in certain past tenses, the others being borrowed from the equivalent, G3700 and G3708; properly to see (literally or figuratively); by implication (in the perfect only) to know: - be aware, behold, X can (+ not tell), consider, (have) known (-ledge), look (on), perceive, see, be sure, tell, understand, wist, wot. δεῖ, dei, die, deh-on' Third person singular active present of G1210; also δεόν deon which is neuter active participle of the same; both used impersonally; it is (was, etc.) necessary (as binding): - behoved, be meet, must (needs), (be) need (-ful), ought, should.

As we have discussed earlier, that statement has led many to believe that the disciples saw an empty mummy wrap, much like a cocoon. That of course would not fit Jewish burial custom. Furthermore, it would also eliminate the need for the return of the women to the tomb to anoint the body. It is admittedly conjecture, but perhaps John remembered at that juncture that Yeshua had already been anointed for burial and described it as such.

Mark 14:3–9 "And while Yeshua was in Bethany at the house of Simon ha-Metzora, reclining at the table, a woman came with an alabaster jar of very expensive oil of pure nard. Breaking open the jar, she poured it over His head. But some got angry and said among themselves, "Why was this fragrant oil wasted? It could have been sold for over three hundred denarii, and the money given to the poor!" And they kept scolding her. But Yeshua said, "Leave her alone. Why do you cause trouble for her? She's done Me a mitzvah. For you always have the poor with you, and you can do good for them whenever you want; but you won't always have Me. She did what she could—she came beforehand to anoint My body for burial. Amen, I tell you, wherever the Good News is proclaimed in all the world, what she has done will also be told in memory of her." TLV

As the Shroud is clearly a burial garment and under normal circumstances would have been considered unclean, *why* in this case was this particular burial cloth kept? Furthermore, is there any historical information pertaining to such a cloth being known prior to the first documented showing of the cloth we now call the Shroud of Turin in Lirey, France circa 1357? British historian, Ian Wilson first broached this very topic in his seminal work, The Shroud of Turin (Doubleday, 1978). Wilson postulates an historical theory that traces the journey of the Shroud first from Jerusalem to Edessa in Turkey where it is described in the Doctrine of Addai[12] as a "mysterious portrait" of Christ. King Abgar V is cured of a disease and converts to Christianity. The cloth remains in Edessa from its arrival until 944 AD when it is handed over to a Bishop sent by the Emperor of Constantinople. During its sojourn in Edessa, due to persecution, it was sealed in a wall above the Western Gate of the city from approximately 57 AD to 525 AD, when a serious flood damaged walls and major buildings. It is without question identified as the cloth brought by Addai. Not only does the fame of this cloth spread far and wide,

12   Ian Wilson, **The Shroud of Turin**, (New York: Doubleday, 1978) pp. 86–125

but from this point (525 AD) onward images of Christ in art bear a striking similarity to this cloth because it is considered to be the authoritative image of Yeshua. In fact, Wilson goes on to point out some fifteen "peculiarities" found on the Shroud and also in artistic renderings of Christ. Citing just two of those paintings, Wilson found thirteen of the fifteen "oddities" which represents an eighty percent congruence. The cloth is alternatively called the "Image of Edessa," the "Mandylion" and the "image not made with hands": Acheiropoietos. The image became famous and spread to many cultures since it was thought to be the legitimate image of Yeshua.[13] In the Eastern Orthodox and Catholic Church, the traditions concerning the Mandylion are well known. One of the most concise renditions of the story is by Taylor Marshall.

---

13   IBID pp. 178–179 incl. photos inserts

Mandylion

According to tradition, King Abgar of Edessa wrote a letter to our Lord Jesus Christ, asking Christ to cure him. King Abgar received a letter in reply from Jesus declining the invitation, but promising a future visit by one of his Apostles (who turns out to be Saint Jude Thaddeus). Eusebius of Caesarea, writing in the 300s, recounts the story for us. He claims that the original letters are still preserved in the city of Edessa. In this version, Christ sends Saint Jude Thaddeus to heal the king. However, a later version of the legend from the 6th century (Acts of Thaddeus) recounts that the image was a "sindon" (Greek for burial shroud), and that it was folded "tetradiplon" (Greek "tetra" = four and "diplon" = twofold). So then, it was a shroud folded twice and then fourfold. Oddly enough, the Holy Shroud of Turin has the exact same fourfold pattern.

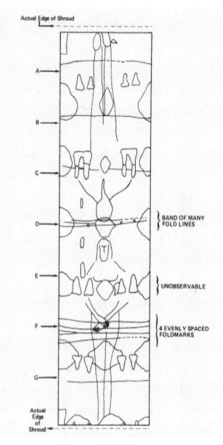

Shroud Folds

This miraculous sindon was given to the King of Edessa along with the letter of Christ. The king was then healed. The letter and Holy Mandylion/ Shroud were kept as prized treasures. Saint John Damascene also described the Holy Image of Edessa as a large garment and not as a small napkin. Where is the Holy Mandylion now? Evagrius Scholasticus, writing about AD 600, reports that a miraculous image of Christ's face was processed around the city of Edessa before the attack of the Persians in 544. The citizens of Edessa attributed their deliverance to the miraculous power of Christ's image.

At the Seventh Ecumenical Council (AD 787), the bishops defended the veneration of images by teaching that Christ Himself provided an image for veneration, namely the Holy Image of Edessa! On August 16, 944, the Holy Image of Edessa was transferred from Edessa to Constantinople. The Eastern Churches consequently keep the feast of the Holy Mandylion on August 16. The Archdeacon of Constantinople, Gregory Referendarius, mentioned in his sermon for the occasion that the image also bore the "side wound" of Christ. This detail indicates that the image transferred from Edessa to Constantinople in 944 was an image of the entire body of Christ. This has led many to conclude that the image in question is the Holy Shroud of Turin. In confirmation of this suspicion, the Emperor Constantine VII, who personally inspected the Edessa image in 944, described the image as "extremely faint, more like a moist secretion without pigment or the painter's art" (Narration de Imagine Edessena). This detail of a "faint image" also suggests that it may be the Holy Shroud of Turin.[14]

---

14   Dr. Taylor Marshall, **How the Shroud of Turin Relates to the Ancient Image of Edessa,** - http://taylormarshall.com/?s=Image+of+Edessa&submit=Search pp.1–8

Edessa Image

The fold pattern has been scientifically confirmed by STURP which lends weight to the theory that the Shroud and the Mandylion are one and the same. That identification would fill in most of the missing years of the Shroud's history and at the same time give an entirely reasonable path from Jerusalem to Lirey, France. Furthermore, that path has already been confirmed by the pollen analysis of the late Max Frei.[15] And the oddities found in so many of the artistic renditions bear striking significance in that the artists themselves were looking directly at the Shroud image.

---

15 Kenneth Stevenson & Gary Habermas, **Verdict on the Shroud**, (Michigan: Servant Press, 1981) pp. 26, 62

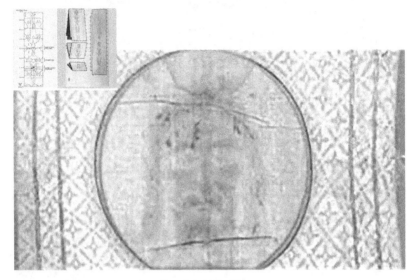

Doubled in Four

Indeed the face and even the body image in art works begin to take on a striking similarity to the Shroud after its arrival in Constantinople where French Crusader Knight Robert De Clari, who recounts his visit during his Chronicle of the Fourth Crusade, said this of what he called the *"sydoines:"* "…about the other marvels that are there [in Constantinople], we shall leave off telling you; for no man on earth, however long he might live in the city, could number them or recount them to you, if any one should recount to you the hundredth part of the richness and the beauty and the splendor [lit. nobility] which was in the abbeys and the churches and in the palaces and in the city, it would seem that it were a lie and you would not believe. And among those other there was another church [lit. another of the churches] which was called My Lady Saint Mary of Blachernae, *where there was the SYDOINES in which [lit. where] Our Lord had been wrapped, which every Friday, raised itself upright, so that one could see the form of our Lord on it [lit. there], and no one, either Greek or French, ever knew what became of this SYNDOINES when the city was taken."*[16]

Is it merely a coincidence that the cloth we now call the Shroud of Turin turns up in the purview of another French Crusader Knight, whose family can only say it was a "spoil of war" and that the image on that cloth clearly inspired the likeness of Christ that spread the world over beginning in the 5th century? I think not. But before we leave the topic of the Shroud in Art, there are two more intriguing clues from the art world, that when added to the other evidence, help to make a compelling case for early knowledge of the Shroud.

First of all, as many have pointed out the Pray Codex circa 1192–1195 shows several striking details that evoke the Shroud. 1) Yeshua is shown naked on the burial cloth; a very rare occurrence in art even *after* the knowledge of the Shroud. 2) His hands are crossed over the pelvic area as they are on the Shroud. 3) The burial cloth displays a herringbone pattern similar to the Shroud. 4) There are four tiny circles in the shape of an "L" exactly like the four *"poker holes"* on the Shroud of Turin. Taken together these items speak to not only the existence of the Shroud before its appearance in Lirey, France, but also the belief by the artist involved that these details were important enough to include. Like the oddities that have defined the confirmation of the facial image being known in art, a similar conclusion can be drawn by such unique characteristics being displayed on a burial garment representing Yeshua.[17]

---

16   Peter Dembowski, **Sindon In The Old French Chronicle of Robert De Clari**, (Shroud Spectrum International, 2013), as cited on Shroud.com: http://www. shroud.com/pdfs/ssi02part5.pdf

17   Wilson, **Shroud**, pp. 130–131 including photo inserts

Pray Codex

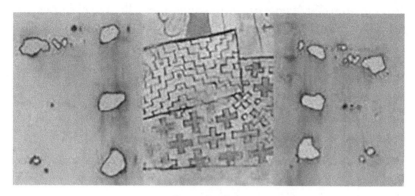

Pray Codex

Art that suggests history

Note: Unusual markings that are found on the Shroud:

Crease in the neck

Box in the forehead

Uneven beard

Hair strands

Facial Oddities

Finally, while visiting Trinity Broadcasting Network's Holy Land Experience in Orlando, Florida, I saw a Russian icon that captured my attention immediately. It is called "*Epitaphoios*" and is used in both Byzantine Catholic and Eastern Orthodox churches during Holy Week to symbolize Christ being laid out in death in the tomb. They also place upon it a "chalice veil" to symbolize the veil in the Tabernacle. Normally, the veil is made from unadorned "*white linen*" or sometimes silk. The oldest extant example is from circa 1200 in Venice, approximately the same time frame as the Pray Codex. The facial features unmistakably mirror the Shroud image. The hands are crossed higher than on the Shroud and a loin cloth has been superimposed. The cloth beneath the body is pure white. The translation of the Russian icon that I saw is as follows: "Yeshua Ha Messiach (Jesus Christ) entered into the new tomb from Joseph the nobleman and was laid down. *Sin was made snow white clean.*"[18]

18   Russian Icon, **Holy Land Experience**, (Orlando, Placard), (Photo)

Epitaphoios

Once again, as has happened several times, just as the book neared completion, an article appeared which strongly supports the Edessan connection. Author Philip F. Dayvault released a new book in February describing his discovery of a first century icon. A tile that was found in Turkey in 2002, and clearly displays the familiar image of all Edessan icons.[19]

The words of the prophet Isaiah and John the Revelator seem extremely pertinent at this point.

> Isaiah 1:18 "Come now, let us reason together," says Adonai. "*Though your sins be like scarlet, they will be as white as snow. Though they be red like crimson, they will become like wool.*" TLV

> Revelation 19:8 "And to her was granted that she should be arrayed in *fine linen, clean and white: for the fine linen is the righteousness of saints.*"

On that note we shall next examine all that Hashem says about *White Linen* and how it relates to the Shroud of Turin.

---

19   Philip Dayvault, **The Keramion-Lost and Found**, (New York: Morgan James Pub., 2016) http://www.kermion502.com (visit directly)

WHITE LINEN

    2 Chronicles 5:12 "Also the Levites *which were* the singers, all of them of Asaph, of Heman, of Jeduthun, with their sons and their brethren, *being* arrayed in *white linen*, having cymbals and psalteries and harps, stood at the east end of the altar, and with them an hundred and twenty priests sounding with trumpets:"

    Revelation 19:8 "And to her was granted that she should be arrayed in fine *linen*, clean and *white*: for the fine linen is the righteousness of saints."

The word "linen" appears in Scripture over one hundred times, nearly always as "fine linen" or "fine twined linen." While the term "white linen," per se, only appears fifteen times, the words translated as "linen" nearly always imply "white linen."

Shêsh, sheshîy, שֵׁשׁ shaysh, shesh-ee´ (The second form for alliteration with H4897); for H7893; *bleached* stuff, that is *white* linen or (by analogy) marble: - X blue, fine [(twined])] linen, marble, silk. בּוּץ, bûwts, boots; from an unused root (of the same form) meaning to *bleach*, that is, (intransitively) *be white*; probably *cotton* (of some sort): - fine (white) linen. Sindôn, *sin-done'* – of uncertain (perhaps foreign) origin; byssos, βύσσος, bussos, *boos'-sos,* of Hebrew origin [H948]; white *linen*: - fine linen.

Since the process of creating linen garments normally included bleaching, and even the most common Greek word for linen came from the Hebrew, it seems logical to conclude that linen garments were generally white.

The first use of the exact phrase "white linen" appears in 2Chronicles 5:12 and in order to understand the significance we shall use Biblical hermeneutics. Hermeneutics is defined as the science and art of Biblical interpretation. Science, because it has an orderly system of specific rules to be used in the interpretation of Biblical texts. Art, because the rules are to be applied in a way that recognizes that communication is flexible and not rigid. Such an understanding would recognize, for example, the use of literary devices in Scripture such as simile and metaphor. For our chosen example we shall use the principle of first mention. According to the principle of first mention, G-d connects the truth concerning a subject in the first mention of that subject.

In context then, the first mention of the phrase "white linen" is rich with significance.

> 2 Chronicles 5: 1-14 "Thus all the work that Solomon made for the house of the LORD was finished: and Solomon brought in *all* the things that David his father had dedicated; and the silver, and the gold, and all the instruments, put he

among the treasures of the house of God. Then Solomon assembled the elders of Israel, and all the heads of the tribes, the chief of the fathers of the children of Israel, unto Jerusalem, to bring up the ark of the covenant of the LORD out of the city of David, which *is* Zion. Wherefore all the men of Israel assembled themselves unto the king in the feast which *was* in the seventh month. And all the elders of Israel came; and the Levites took up the ark. And they brought up the ark, and the tabernacle of the congregation, and all the holy vessels that *were* in the tabernacle, these did the priests *and* the Levites bring up. Also king Solomon, and all the congregation of Israel that were assembled unto him before the ark, sacrificed sheep and oxen, which could not be told nor numbered for multitude. And the priests brought in the ark of the covenant of the LORD unto his place, to the oracle of the house, into the most holy *place, even* under the wings of the cherubims: For the cherubims spread forth *their* wings over the place of the ark, and the cherubims covered the ark and the staves thereof above. And they drew out the staves *of the ark*, that the ends of the staves were seen from the ark before the oracle; but they were not seen without. And there it is unto this day. *There was* nothing in the ark save the two tables which Moses put *therein* at Horeb, when the LORD made *a covenant* with the children of Israel, when they came out of Egypt. And it came to pass, when the priests were come out of the holy *place*: (for all the priests *that were* present were sanctified, *and* did not *then* wait by course: Also the Levites *which were* the singers, all of them of Asaph, of Heman, of Jeduthun, with their sons and their brethren, b*eing* arrayed in *white linen*, having cymbals and psalteries and harps, stood at the east end of the altar, and with them an hundred and twenty priests sounding with trumpets.) It came even to pass, as the trumpeters and singers *were* as one, to make one sound to be heard in praising and thanking the LORD; and when they lifted up *their* voice with the trumpets and cymbals and instruments of musick, and praised the LORD, *saying,* For *he is* good; for his mercy *endureth* for ever: that *then* the house was filled with a cloud, *even* the house of the LORD; So that the priests could not stand to minister by reason of the cloud: for the glory of the LORD had filled the house of God."

King Solomon had completed the Temple, and the Ark, (which represents the very presence of G-d) and it has been brought into the Holy of Holies. Now, the priests and Levites all clothed in *"white linen"* stand at the east end of the altar sounding the shofars and when they lift up their voices and instruments in one accord the very Glory of G-d fills the house and no one can stand in His presence. What must not be lost from the picture are two phrases that may provide a key to the purpose of the Shroud.

2 Chronicles 5:6 "Also king Solomon, and all the congregation of Israel that were assembled unto him before the ark, sacrificed sheep and oxen, which could not be told nor numbered for multitude."

2 Chronicles 5:11 "And it came to pass, when the priest were come out of the holy *place*: (for all the priests *that were* present were sanctified, *and* did not *then* wait by course..."

Having sacrificed a multitude of sheep and oxen, surely the white linen garments were stained with blood. Furthermore, the presence of Hashem descends after the priests exit the Holy Place and we know they would sprinkle the people with the sacrificial blood according to Leviticus 16 and 17. More importantly, when we read that: "And it came to pass, when the priests where come out of the holy *place*: (for all the priests *that were* present were sanctified, *and* did not *then* wait by course:" does it not call to mind the promise of Hashem to Moishe concerning *all* the people?

> Exodus 19:6 "And ye shall be unto me a *kingdom of priests*, and an holy nation. These *are* the words which thou shalt speak unto the children of Israel."

Furthermore, in the Book of Revelation (the disclosure; revealing; manifestation) John twice paints a very similar picture for us to find:

> Revelation 7:9–11 "After this I beheld, and, lo, a great multitude, which no man could number, of all nations, and kindreds, and people, and tongues, stood before the throne, and before the Lamb, *clothed with white robes*, and palms in their hands; And cried with a loud voice, saying, salvation to our God which sitteth upon the throne, and unto the Lamb. And all the angels stood round about the throne, and *about* the elders and the four beats, and fell before the throne on their faces, and worshipped God," (Emphasis added)

> Revelation 7:13–14 "And one of the elders answered, saying unto me, What are these which are

arrayed in white robes? And whence came they? And I said unto him, Sir, thou knowest. And he said to me, These are they which came out of great tribulation, and *have washed their robes, and made them white in the blood of the Lamb*." (Emphasis added)

Revelation 19:7–8 "Let us be glad and rejoice, and give honour to him: for the marriage of the Lamb is come, and his wife hath made herself ready. And to her was granted *that she should be arrayed in fine linen, clean and white: for the fine linen is the righteousness of saints.*" (Emphasis added)

Revelation 19:13–14 "And he *was* clothed *with a vesture dipped in blood: and his name is called The Word of God. And the armies which were in heaven followed him upon white horses, clothed in fine linen, white and clean.*" (Emphasis added)

In each case there are white line garments that are washed in blood, and in the case of the "Word of G-D," dipped in blood. Both events are connected to worship at the very throne of Hashem. Perhaps most telling in this case are the following two factors: first that the "blood of the Lamb" made the robes "white" and secondly that the "white linen" is equated to "righteousness."

Leviticus 14:25 "And he shall kill *the lamb* of the trespass offering, and the priest shall take *some of the blood of the trespass offering, and put it upon the tip of the right ear of him that is to be cleansed*, and upon the thumb of his right hand, and upon the great toe of his right foot:" (Emphasis added)

Or, as Paul says in Hebrews:

> Hebrews 9:22 "And almost *all things are by the law purged with blood; and without shedding of blood is no remission."* (Emphasis added)

There is clearly, throughout the Word of Hashem, a pivotal role played by "linen." Angels wear linen (Ezekiel, Daniel, and Revelation), the priests wear linen (Exodus, Leviticus), and the promise of G-D to the saints is connected to linen (Revelation 19):

> Revelation 19:8 "And to her was granted that she should be arrayed in fine linen, clean and white: for the fine linen is the righteousness of saints."

In the book of Exodus, linen plays an important role in the construction of the tabernacle in the wilderness, as well as the manufacture of the priestly garments. Perhaps the most important being the veil which covered the entrance to the holy of holies.

> Exodus 26:31–33 "And thou shalt make a vail *of* blue, and purple, and scarlet, and fine twined linen of cunning work: with cherubims shall it be made: And thou shalt hang it upon four pillars of shittim *wood* overlaid with gold: their hooks *shall be of* gold, upon the four sockets of silver. And thou shalt hang up the vail under the taches, that thou mayest bring in thither within the vail the ark of the testimony: and the vail shall divide unto you between the holy *place* and the most holy."

The very veil which would be rent from top to bottom when Adonai Yeshua Ha Messiach offered Himself as the final sacrifice.

> Mark 15:37–38 "And Jesus cried with a loud voice, and gave up the ghost. And the veil of the temple was rent in twain from the top to the bottom."

And while Mark does not tell us what Yeshua cried at that point, John does.

> John 19:30 "When Jesus therefore had received the vinegar, he said, *It is finished*: and he bowed his head, and gave up the ghost." (Emphasis added)

The Lamb slain from the foundation of the world declares the completion of the payment of our collective "sin debt" with those three words, and the way is once again made for open fellowship with Hashem. Teléō, τελέω, *tel-eh'-o*, from G5056; to *end*, that is *complete, execute, conclude, discharge* (a debt): accomplish, make an end, expire, fill up, finish, go over, pay, perform.

In the book of Esther, there is a hidden reference to "white linen" that also has a direct connection to the Passover. As we mentioned in chapter one, "karpas" used as an "appetizer" in the Seder meal appears **once** in the entire Bible: Esther 1:6. However, as we learned, it is from the Persian word "kirpas" meanings "white linen." Moreover, contextually, it has been connected with the rite of marking the door with the "blood of the lamb." "...Vegetables in salt water...to remind of the branch of hyssop dipped in blood to mark the outlines of doors of Israelite houses in Egypt = "placed under protection." In the same commentary, the term "karpas" is said to represent a doorway, a passage and the Hebrew to be a passer who is "becoming…not just the certitude of the Messiah," but a "way of being."[20]

Surely the convergence of white linen, the blood of the lamb, and a Passover ritual aligning with a "Messianic becoming: speaks volumes at this juncture. Even more so since it is connected to a door. However, there is still more to cover where linen is concerned.

Christian tradition has long utilized "altar linens" in worship services. Perhaps many would not know that this long standing tradition is actually directly connected to the burial linens of Yeshua. In his brief but masterful paper on this subject, the late Reverend Albert R. Dreisbach, Jr. not only took this tradition back to 325 A.D., but also linked it directly to the Shroud's sojourn in Edessa and Constantinople. Furthermore, he references the connection to the original disciples in their mission to carry the Gospel to that region. "As early as A.D. 325 during a council at the Baths of Trajan, Pope Sylvester with the Emperor Constantine and 327 bishops in attendance established: that *the holy sacrifice of the Mass be celebrated on a cloth of linen consecrated* by the Bishop, *as if it were the clean Shroud of Christ* [Emphasis added] (Labbe, Scr. Conc., p. 1542. Cited by G. Ricci, *Guide to the Photographic Exhibit of the Holy Shroud* (Milwaukee: Center for the Study of the Passion of Christ and the Holy Shroud (1982), p. XX)." Pregnant with potential implications by and for the Shroud is the following brief quote from the Hymn itself: "The [splendid robe] became like me, as my reflection in a mirror [Note: the "reversed image" on the Shroud as if it were a photographic negative.], And

---

20 Haggadah Commentary

in it saw myself [quite] apart from myself, so that we were two in distinction and again one in single form (*Hymn 76–78…*). "[21]

"A splendid robe which shows a reflection in a mirror?"

Returning to the fourth century, Theordore of Mopsuesta (ca. A.D. 350–428) takes us beyond Ephraim of Odessa when—in describing the liturgy—he notes in his *Cateches* that the deacons: "When they bring up (the oblation at the offertory) they place it on the altar for the completed representation of the passion so that we may think of Him on the altar as if He were placed in the sepulcher after having received the passion. This is why the deacons who spread the linens on the altar *represent the figure of the linen cloths at the burial* [Emphasis added] {Cited by Dom Gregory Dix. *The Shape of the Liturgy* (London: Dacre, 1960) p. 282)}.[22] Not only do we have mention of a *figure* on *linen*; but that *figure* is specifically identified as a *post*-passion image of Jesus on the linen burial cloths in the sepulcher.

While surfing the internet for information on linen, I discovered www.zipporahsthimble.com. It is a website of Zipporah Reshel Designs (set apart garments of righteousness). Her primary Scripture reference immediately caught my attention: Isaiah 52:1. We will discuss this reference in-depth in the chapter *Startled and Sprinkled*, however, in short, it calls for Zion to awaken and don *beautiful garments*. Not only are the linen garments created by Reshel indeed beautiful, but on her website she details many spiritually and scientifically significant aspects of linen. "Since the earliest times, flax has been known to have healing properties.

---

21   Rev. Albert R. Dreisbach, **Thomas & the Hymn of the Pearl**, (Georgia: AICCST, 2000) p.14

22   Rev. Albert R. Dreisbach, **Liturgical Clues to the Shroud's History**, (Georgia: AICSST, 1995)

Recent studies out of Japan and posted from the linen textile manufacturers confirm this truth. In the Latin language, the word flax means "being most useful" and the Holy Scriptures certainly emphasized this material over all other fabrics for the Holy attire. The original Hebrew language gives the attire of Adam and Even as a linen robe of light (Genesis 3:21). In establishing the protocols 'statutes' of health, the prophet Moses received specific instructions. Cleansing a 'leper' meaning those 'incurable' gave only three distinct fabrics of attire: wool or linen or leather (Leviticus 13:47–48). It was emphasized as forbidden to wear linen and wool together (Leviticus 19:19 and Deuteronomy 22:11). Historically, the beautiful white linen attire of the Hebrew people was with Almighty God's specific instructions, the decisions as given in the instructions 'Torah' as ordinances (Exodus 39:1–31). What special qualities were in this linen material that would restore life? Comprising a multitude of household items, flax fabric is an excellent filter protecting against chemical exposure, noise and dust. Linen clothing reduces solar gamma radiation by almost half thereby protecting humans wearing linen. Flax fiber retrieved from contaminated soil appears to be totally resistant to harmful radiation. Linen underwear heightens positive emotions as well as possessing rare bacteriological properties. Resistant to fungus and bacteria, flax is found to be an effective barrier to some diseases."[23]

Once again, as I have found throughout this study, the story of "linen" in Scripture, as seen manifested by the Shroud, fulfills in type the promise, pattern and prophecy of Hashem. It is now time to investigate the meaning of Nazah: "*Startled and Sprinkled.*"

---

23   Hebrews Today, as cited by Zipporah Reshel, **Linen: The Preferred Fabric for Clothing of Healing, Healthy Living and Well Being**, Hebrews Today: (California 2006), http://www.zipporahsthimble.com/Linen_Info.html

STARTLED AND SPRINKLED

Isaiah 29:10 "For the LORD hath poured out upon you the spirit of deep sleep, and hath closed your eyes: the prophets and your rulers, the seers hath he covered."

Psalms 17:15 "As for me, I will behold thy face in righteousness: I shall be satisfied, when I awake, with thy likeness."

Isaiah chapter 52, is for me, a pivotal Messianic chapter with clear ties to the Shroud of Turin. Taken in context, this powerful Messianic chapter begins with a cry from Isaiah for Zion to awaken, put on beautiful garments and publish "salvation" (Yeshua).

Isaiah 52:1–3 "Awaken, awake; put on thy strength, O Zion; put on thy beautiful garments, O Jerusalem, the holy city: for henceforth there shall no more come into thee the uncircumcised and the unclean. Shake thyself from the dust; arise, *and* sit down, O Jerusalem: loose thyself from the bands of thy neck, O captive daughter of Zion. For thus saith the LORD, Ye have sold yourselves for nought; and ye shall be redeemed without money."

Isaiah 52:6–7 "Therefore my people shall know my name: therefore *they shall know* in that day that I *am* he that doth speak: behold, *it is* I. How beautiful upon the mountains are the feet of him that bringeth good tidings, that publisheth peace; that bringeth good tidings of good, that publisheth salvation (Yeshua); that saith unto Zion, Thy God reigneth!"

Next, Isaiah takes us to a time of rejoicing: the restoration of Zion and the redemption of Jerusalem. Then he declares that the Lord will uncover His Holy arm to the nations and the ends of the earth shall see His salvation (Yeshua).

Isaiah 52:8–10 "Thy watchmen shall lift up the voice; with the voice together shall they sing: for they shall see eye to eye, when the LORD shall bring again Zion. Break forth into joy, sing together, ye wasted

places of Jerusalem: for the LORD hath comforted his people, he hath redeemed Jerusalem. The LORD hath made bare his holy arm in the eyes of all the nations; and all the ends of the earth shall see the salvation (Yeshua) of our God."

Which brings us to the passage that started me on this quest: Isaiah 52:13–15.

Isaiah 52:13–15 "Behold, my servant shall deal prudently, he shall be exalted and extolled, and be very high. As many were astonied at thee; his visage was so marred more than any man, and his form more than the sons of men: So shall he sprinkle many nations; the kings shall shut their mouths at him: for *that* which had not been told them shall they see; and *that* which they had not heard shall they consider."

(See Photo #6, the Blood Image)

The Hebrew word "Nazah," which is rendered "sprinkle" in Isaiah 52:15 appears in the Torah twenty-four times. (A significance we shall address later.) According to the a) Strong's and b) BDB respectively, it means: b) 1) to spurt, spatter, sprinkle 1a) (Qal) to spurt, spatter b) (Hiphil) to cause to spurt, sprinkle upon 2) to spring, leap 2a) (Hiphil) to cause to leap, *startle*. (Emphasis added.)

Isaiah makes the statement that the marred face and body of Hashem's exalted, extolled servant would startle and sprinkle many nations. Further, that they would see it even though they had never been told. The Scripture then adds the fact that they would consider what they had never even heard about. Once again we consult a) Strong's and b) BDB for the term "consider:" A) *bene*; a primitive root; to *separate* mentally (or *distinguish*), that is (generally) *understand*: - attend, consider, be cunning, diligently, direct, discern, eloquent, feel, inform, instruct, have intelligence, know, look well to, mark, perceive, be prudent, regard, (can) skill (-ful), teach, think, (cause, make to, get, give, have) understand (-ing), view, (deal) wise (-ly, man). B) 1) to discern, understand, consider 1a) (Qal) 1a1) to perceive, discern 1a2) to understand, know (with the mind) 1a3) to observe, mark, give heed to, distinguish, consider 1a4) to have discernment, insight, understanding 1b) (Niphal) to be discerning, intelligent, discreet, have understanding 1c) (Hiphil) 1c1) to understand 1c2) to cause to understand, give understanding, teach 1d) (Hithpolel) to show oneself discerning or attentive, consider diligently 1e) (Polel) to teach, instruct 2) (TWOT) prudent, regard.

The prophet Isaiah declares they would discern, observe, teach, and understand it even though they had never heard about it. The implication is that of a startling future manifestation of this exalted, suffering servant that could be seen, studied and considered diligently: a manifestation that would "sprinkle" its witnesses with the blood of expiation.

Since the Scripture tells us to "seek His face" several times (e.g. 2 Chronicles 7:14; Psalms 27:8; Psalms 105:4; Hosea 5:15) and Isaiah plainly states that Hashem did not tell us "in vain" to seek Him, can this image be the "human *face*" of Yahweh's Yeshua (salvation) marred more than *any* man, to reveal His redemption to *all* men?

> Isaiah 45:19 "I have not spoken in secret, in a dark place of the earth: I said not unto the seed of Jacob, Seek ye me in vain: I the LORD speak righteousness, I declare things that are right."

Nor is the prophet Isaiah alone in such a startling proclamation that involves seeing the One who purchases our redemption. The prophet Zechariah has equally significant prophecies that can clearly be connected to the Shroud.

> Zechariah 12:10 "And I will pour upon the house of David, and upon the inhabitants of Jerusalem, the spirit of grace and of supplications: and they shall look upon me whom they have pierced, and they shall mourn for him, as one mourneth for *his* only *son*, and shall be in bitterness for him, as one that is in bitterness for *his* firstborn."

> Zechariah 13:1, 6 "In that day there shall be a fountain opened to the house of David and to the inhabitants of Jerusalem for sin and for uncleanness." "And *one* shall say unto him, what *are* these wounds in thine hands? Then he shall answer, *those* with which I was wounded *in* the house of my friends."

In this case, the word "pierced" means "stabbed" or "struck through." Dâqar, *daw-kar'* A primitive root; to *stab*; by analogy to *starve*; figuratively to *revile* - pierce, strike (thrust) through, wound. Once again, there is a direct correlation to the wounds of the man of the Shroud: a stab wound to the side and wounds to the hands as well.

It makes sense at this point to note that the three major monotheistic religions are all awaiting the arrival of a great spiritual leader. The need for that arrival made more apparent daily by a world seemingly bent on self-destruction. However, the arrival anticipated by each should be a cause for open rejoicing as they each expect a ruler who will establish a "theocracy" for planet Earth. Why then does Zechariah say G-d's people will mourn bitterly? Furthermore, why also does he prophesy that they will "look upon" one who "they" have pierced and question the "wounds" in his hands? Is it merely a coincidence that the Shroud would logically answer all these questions and in these last days be yet another literal fulfillment of Scripture? Christians and Messianic believers alike have seen such wounds in art and film, and indeed as is reported of both "Jesus of Nazareth" and "The Passion of the Christ" many have wept and mourned openly the death of the Messiah as depicted on film. Nevertheless, Zechariah states twice that *this* prophecy pertains to the house of David and the inhabitants of Jerusalem.

Most recently I reached out to several Messianic organizations about this research and was surprised to be rejected out of hand without any chance to even present the mounting evidence. In my opinion, that moves the ultimate fulfillment of that prophecy to an as yet future day. Meanwhile, there is clear evidence in the Christian Scriptures to suggest this process began in the days immediately following the crucifixion, *but* that there is yet a major fulfillment to come.

Before His passion and death, which He explained in detail, Yeshua also accurately prophesied what would happen when He was taken. In fact, He cited from the same Zechariah passage we just looked at.

> Zechariah 13:7 "Awake, O sword, against my shepherd, and against the man *that is* my fellow, saith the LORD of hosts: smite the shepherd, and the sheep shall be scattered: and I will turn mine hand upon the little ones."

Matthew 26:31 "Then Yeshua said to them, "This night you will all fall away because of Me; for it is written, 'I will strike the Shepherd, and the sheep of the flock will be scattered.'" TLV

Matthew 26:56 "But all this was done, that the scriptures of the prophets might be fulfilled. *Then all the disciples forsook him, and fled."* (Emphasis added)

The disciples fled and even denied knowing Yeshua for fear of being taken with Him. They were totally demoralized by what had happened. Only Joseph of Arimathaea and Nicodemus took care to retrieve and bury the body. Yet what a dramatic change occurs after the disciples visit the tomb.

John 20:1–9 "The first *day* of the week cometh Mary Magdalene early, when it was yet dark, unto the sepulchre, and seeth the stone taken away from the sepulchre. Then she runneth, and cometh to Simon Peter, and to the other disciple, whom Jesus loved, and saith unto them, They have taken away the Lord out of the sepulchre, and we know not where they have laid him. Peter therefore went forth, and that other disciple, and came to the sepulchre. So they ran both together: and the other disciple did outrun Peter, and came first to the sepulchre. And he stooping down, *and looking in*, saw the linen clothes lying; yet went he not in. Then cometh Simon Peter following him, and went into the sepulchre, and seeth the linen clothes lie, And the napkin, that was about his head, not lying with linen clothes, but wrapped together in a place by itself. Then went in also that other disciple, which came first to the sepulchre, and *he saw, and believed.* For as yet they knew not the scripture that he must rise again from the dead."

Here begins the most incredible part of the story. John, who reaches the tomb first, does not enter until Peter goes in. However, when John does go in, the report is amazing: "…he saw and believed…" even though he "knew not the scripture that he must rise again from the dead." The Greek language here is so strong a statement it has caused researchers to ponder what exactly he "saw" in that empty tomb. Sadly, for the most part they reach the untenable conclusion that there was an empty mummy case, through which the body of Yeshua must have passed. That as we know for certain is *not* in keeping with Jewish burial customs, which leaves the question unanswered as to what John saw that convinced him of the resurrection rather than a stolen body.

A few years ago while traveling to speak on the Shroud, I caught a glimpse of a book by Thomas de Wesselow entitled, "THE SIGN: The Shroud of Turin and the Secret of the Resurrection" which bore both the negative and positive images of the face and quoted this same Scripture. I purchased the book immediately but within only a few of its 450 pages realized that he did not believe in a literal resurrection and so I shelved it. However, as I was in the process of writing this book, I was strongly impressed to get the book down and read it. What became clear only a few pages further in than I had read before was that the author was *convinced* that the image itself, as it appears on the Shroud, was what persuaded the disciples and later Paul that Yeshua had indeed risen from the dead. Something took these men from timidly hiding behind closed doors to openly embracing the resurrection even to their own martyrdom. Furthermore, in the case of Paul, as we shall see, he gives tantalizing clues as to what he knew about the empty tomb and fulfilled prophecy.

Brushing aside the account of the empty tomb, de Wesselow builds an exceptionally strong case for the image *alone* being, in the disciples' minds, *proof* of the resurrection. Perhaps the most important factor for me in reading his book was the use of non-canonical references that he was able to assemble that clearly point to the image on the Shroud. Although I had known some of them previously, there were at least an equal amount that were new. One of the most significant is a reference he found in a liturgical text from the "sixth or seventh century."

"… (a) liturgical text known as the Mozarabic Rite… tells how 'Peter ran with John to the tomb and saw the recent traces (vestigia) of the dead and risen man in the linen cloths." de Wesselow concludes that this and other early writings clearly refer to the "imprint on the Shroud." He also connects it to other apocryphal writings from the same time period when the Shroud was likely known as the Mandylion and had already been transferred from Edessa to Constantinople. (See the chapter *The Shroud in Art.*) Focusing on the "Doctrine of Addai" de Wesselow sets about to make the case first mentioned by Ian Wilson that the Shroud was brought to Edessa sometime in the First Century. Basing his opinion on the supposition that "Thomas" was a nickname meaning "twin" de Wesselow decides that Judas (Jude) was Thomas and responsible for the establishment of the church in Edessa. However, according to Scripture Thomas, which does in fact mean "the twin" was also called Didymus which also means "double or twin."[24]

---

24   Thomas De Wesselow, **The Sign: The Shroud of Turin and the Secret of the Resurrection**, (New York: Dutton, 2012) pp. 326–327

Thōmas, *tho-mas'*: of Chaldee origin (compare [H8380]); *the twin*; *Thomas*, a Christian – Thomas.

Didumos, *did'-oo-mos*: Prolonged from G1364; *double*, that is, *twin*; *Didymus*, a Christian: - Didymus.

However, during my own research for historical evidence I long ago discovered "The Search For The Twelve Apostle" by William S. McBirnie, in which Jude is called Jude "trinomious" (of three names). The names were Jude, Thaddeus and Lebbaeus, rather than Thomas or Diduymus.[25] According to most scholars, Jude and Thomas, at some point, ministered together in Edessa. Also, Jude is connected with the Image of Edessa (Mandylion) and frequently shown with that image in a circular frame. Furthermore, Jude Thaddeus is also known historically as Mar Addai, clearly linking him back to the Doctrine of Addai. ("Mar" is the ancient word denoting "a bishop.")

After making the case for some four hundred pages, not only that the Shroud is genuine, but also in order to arrive at the conclusion that the Shroud convinced the disciples and Paul of the resurrection and yet still *not himself* believe in a literal bodily resurrection, de Wesselow seizes upon the Greek word "acheiropoietos" translated "not made with hands." The word first appears in Mark 14:58, but Rabbi Paul uses the same description in 2Corinthians 5:1. Acheiropoietos: *akh-i-rop-ay'-ay-tos* ; from G1 (as a negative particle) and G5499; *unmanufactured*, that is, *inartificial*: - made without (not made with) hands.

To acknowledge that the Shroud's enigmatic image was indeed *not made with human hands* clearly implies an event that is unprecedented. That, in my opinion, points to one fundamental conclusion: *the Resurrection*. The disciples never mentioned a body

---

25   William Stuart McBirnie, **The Search For The Twelve Apostles**, (Illinois, Tyndale House, 1973) p. 204

or an unwrapping of the same, and there is no evidence of the type of ablation you would expect from unwrapping, given the severe damage to the body. To point out the obvious, if the body were still in the cloth, you could not possibly see the image. If the body remained in the cloth, Mary would not have asked, "Where have you laid him?"

In view of all of these things, de Wesselow's conclusions are very telling and significant. "...if the Shroud is an authentic relic of the burial of Jesus (Yeshua), as it would seem to be, it should be recognized as an essential historical source. Until now it has been considered normal and acceptable for New Testament scholars to ignore the Shroud, but this attitude neither was nor is justified. The Shroud counts against any resurrection theory that denies the basic historicity of the tomb-stories... It undermines any theory involving body-theft...it disproves the "swoon theory" *The Shroud...is nothing less than the image of the Risen Christ...*"[26]

His last statement sounds very much like the title of my last Shroud book, "The Image of the Risen Christ." The fact of the matter is when you know the whole truth concerning the Shroud it is indeed *"startling!"* It is my considered opinion, having seen the extremes to which men will go to deny the obvious where the Shroud is concerned, that men are so startled by the truth that they will go to any length rather than to accept the plain truth.

A wise man once said if you want to hide something put it in a book. Next we shall examine how the truths wrapped in the Shroud were hidden in plain sight in the Book of books, the Word of God all along.

---

26   De Wesselow, **The Sign**, pp. 341–342

HIDDEN IN PLAIN SIGHT

Proverbs 25:2 "It is the glory of God to conceal a thing: but the honour of kings *is* to search out a matter."

The very construct of this Proverb is significant and apropos to our study of the Shroud. The word translated "glory" and the word translated "honour" are the same. It is the Hebrew word "kabod" which, according to Strong's definition is: kâbôd, כָּבֹד; כָּבוֹד *kaw-bode', kaw-bode'* from H3513; properly *weight*; but only figuratively in a good sense, *splendor* or *copiousness*; glorious (-ly), glory, honour (-able). BDB Definition: glory, honour, glorious, abundance 1a) abundance, riches 1b) honour, splendor, glory 1c) honour, reputation 1e) honour, reverence, glory 1f) glory.

Likewise, the word translated "thing" is the same as the word translated "matter." In this case, the Hebrew word is "dabar" which Strong's renders: dabar, *daw-bawr'* דָּבָר, from H1696; a *word*; by implication a *matter* (as *spoken* of) of *thing*; adverbially a *cause*: -act, advice, affair, answer, X any such (thing), + because of, book, business, care, case, cause, certain rate, + chronicles, commandment, X commune (-ication), + concern [-ing], + confer, counsel, + dearth, decree, deed, X disease, due, duty, effect, + eloquent, errand, [evil favoured-] ness, + glory, + harm, hurt, + iniquity, + judgment, language, + lying, manner, matter, message, [no] thing, oracle, X ought, X parts, + pertaining, + please, portion, + power, promise, provision, purpose, question, rate, reason, report, request, X (as hast) said, sake, saying, sentence, + sign, + so, some [uncleanness], somewhat to say, + song, speech, X spoken, talk, task, + that, X there done, thing (concerning), thought, + thus, tidings, what [-soever], + wherewith, which, word, work. BDB Definition: 1) speech, word, speaking, thing 1a) speech 1b) saying, utterance 1c) word, words 1d) business, occupation, acts, matter, case, something, manner.

What stands out in this couplet is that "dabar" here translated "thing" and "matter" is most normally translated "word." The first example of which is found when G-d speaks to Abraham.

> Genesis 15–1 "After these things *the word of the LORD* came unto Abram in a vision, saying, Fear not, Abram: I *am* thy shield, *and* thy exceeding great reward."

The logical questions then would be first, why would the Most High conceal His Word, and secondly, since His plan is to make us "kings and priests (Revelation 1:6; 5:10) what "glory" is planned as we "search out" His Word? The meaning of the term used for "search out" is also significant to our study. Châqar, חקר *khaw-kar'* A primitive root; properly to *penetrate*; hence to *examine* intimately: - find out, (make) search (out), seek (out), sound, try, BDB definition: 1) to search, search for, search out, examine, investigate 1a) (Qal) 1a1 to search (for) 1a2) to search through, explore 1a3) to examine thoroughly 1b) (Niphal) 1b1) to be searched out, be found out, be ascertained, be examined 1c) (Piel) to search out, seek out.

The clear implication here is that we are to seek an intimate knowledge of G-d's Word, not simply a surface reading, but a penetration into its depths. As Yeshua declared to those who would be His disciples:

> John 5:38–39 "And ye have not his word abiding in you: for whom he hath sent, him ye believe not. Search the scriptures; for in them ye think ye have eternal life: and they are they which testify of me."

In fact, the search itself is a demonstration of our faith and will be rewarded by Hashem.

> Hebrews 11:6 "But without faith *it is* impossible to please *him*: for he that cometh to God must believe that he is, and *that* he is a rewarder of them that diligently seek him."

For over forty years now, I have been trying to do just that. Searching the Scriptures for clues that might indeed confirm the Shroud of Turin as the actual burial garment worn by Yeshua in the tomb. Along the way, I became fascinated with the discovery of the Torah Codes and purchased the software as soon as it was made commercially available. However, even though there seemed to be numerous ELS (Equidistant Letter Sequences) pointing to the Shroud, I could not seem to find a clear understanding of the significance of those codes. Even the late Grant Jeffrey, an early Codes proponent and publisher of my third Shroud book, *Image of the Risen Christ*, could not provide answers on the numerous codes which I had found.[27]

Russ Breault, founder of "STEP" Shroud of Turin Education Project, Inc. and www.ShroudEncounter.com, a researcher and lecturer on the Shroud of Turin for over 30 years, in March, 2017 shared a passage from Isaiah chapter 26 with the Shroud Science Group (a private online mailing list of scientists, historians and researchers who exchange discussion on scientific aspects related to the Shroud). The implication of the translation is quite remarkable.

> Isaiah 25:6–9 "On this mountain, Adonai-Tzva'ot will prepare a lavish banquet for all people—a banquet of aged wine—of rich food, of choice marrow, of aged wine well refined. On this mountain He will swallow up the shroud that enfolds all peoples, the veil spread over all nations. He will swallow up death forever. My Lord Adonai will wipe away tears from every face. He will remove His people's reproach from all the earth. For Adonai has spoken. It will be said in that day: "Behold, this is our God, we waited for Him—He will save us. This is Adonai—we waited for Him. We will rejoice and be glad in His salvation."" TLV

Russ shared his thought regarding this passage as follows: "…the translation demonstrates Isaiah is referencing a burial

27 Personal Conversation, Grant R. Jeffrey, 1999

shroud covering the entire human race. The entire doctrine of substitutionary atonement can be seen in these verse. It begins with a celebration, a feast, an allusion to the Marriage Supper of the Lamb. "Mountain" is a reference to Zion or the New Jerusalem. He will destroy death AND the burial shroud covering all people… the blood on the Shroud represents the atonement made on our behalf. The image represents His victory over death…there is only one cloth that covers someone in death and that is a shroud…I believe that the Shroud covering Jesus in the tomb represents the shroud of death covering all people that is destroyed or rendered useless through the resurrection. In addition, I think the Shroud now, 2000 years later, is the "sign of the prophet Jonah: which is the only sign that will be given to a "wicked and adulterous generation."

As well, a trusted intercessor and bible researcher from our ministry examined the same verses in Isaiah 25 and based on her study of the root Hebrew words came away with this conclusion: "The vail, the covering over the people is a woven (cloth) that enwraps or enfolds, engulfs, eats up. It also involves the idea of a cast image…God swallows up this image, this face of death and replaces the image of death with His image. He "swallows up" death in this way. The shroud, covering, vail of death that had covered the people, is swallowed up and is now the shroud, vail, covering that bears the image, the face of the King of life."

Another much more promising area of research developed when my son, Kenneth, III began to share with me his knowledge of the Hebrew language as it appears in both the ancient pictographic alphabet, as well as in Modern Hebrew. First of all, as a former English professor, I was always fascinated by the deeper meanings found in the various concordances for the words translated into English from both Greek and Hebrew. As a pastor, it was always rewarding to bring those meanings forth in my teachings of the Bible. In addition, having studied Latin for four years it seemed incredible to me that the only "dead language" ever to be resurrected and used daily in our modern world is Hebrew. Given the fact that what sets the Bible apart is fulfilled prophecy, the restoration of the Hebrew language becomes a momentous historical event.

> Zephaniah 3:9 "For then will I turn to the people a pure language, that they may all call upon the name of the LORD, to serve him with one consent."

The only dead language in the history of Mankind to be resurrected is Hebrew and given that the Torah, as well as the rest of the Hebrew Testament, is written in Hebrew, we stand to attain a better understanding of what the ancient sages actually wrote: what the Ruach Ha Kodesh intended.[28]

Recently, while preparing messages for the High Holy Days, in order to ensure a better understanding of the prophetic significance of the Jewish Feast Days, I discovered a website that opened my eyes to a greater depth in the Hebrew language. The website, www.answersintheendtimes.com while comprised of only a relatively limited number of pages, overall contained intriguing clues to the richness hidden in plain sight in the Ancient Hebrew Pictographs. The very first example of which was the meaning of the phrase "In the beginning," which in the Hebrew, is the word "barasheet." Seen below, beautifully portrayed pictorially, (as found at www.beautfyofthebible.com) translates as:[29]

---

28   J. R. Watts, **Shroud Codes in the Bible**, (New York, Center for Biblical Cryptology), 2016

29   In the Beginning: http://www.answersintheendtimes. com

The son of God consumed his hand on a cross.

| the earth | and | the heavens | ??? | God | created | In the beginning |

ב -BET: House (House/Tent) ⊔

ר -RESH: First Person (Man's Head) ৎ

[Son = בר]

א -ALEPH: God (Ox Head) ⌁

ש -SHIN: Consume/Destroy (Teeth) ⊔⊔

י -YOD: Hand/Works (Hand/Arm) ﮪ

ת -TAV: Covenant/Mark (Cross) †

Barasheet

Put into perspective, it is even confirmed by the final book of the Bible, Revelation:

> Revelation 13:8 "And all that dwell upon the earth shall worship him, whose names are not written in the book of life of *the Lamb slain from the foundation of the world.*" (Aleph Tav, prophetically.)

An even greater revelation was to be found in the Tetragrammaton. The four Hebrew letters of "Yud-Hey-Vav-Hey" that comprise one of the names for G-d Almighty are often referred to by biblical scholars as the "Tetragrammaton" which is merely a Greek term for something with four letters.

Yud Hey Vav Hey
Yud: The Hand and Vav: the Nail

When we consider all of the potential meanings of the individual letters above, there is really only one sensible pattern that emerges that relates to G-d. The potential meanings are included in the chart below. From the pictographs, it is clear that G-d is conveying the following revelation, which in our English construct, would be stated as:

"Behold the Hand, Behold the Nail."

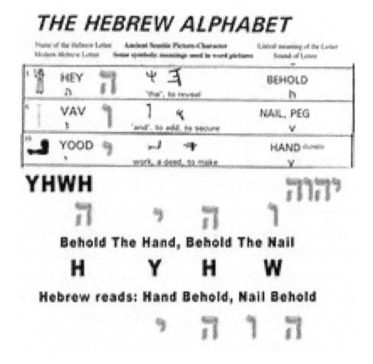

Behold the Hand

There, in the very name of G-d Himself, we find the prophecy of our Elohim, Yeshua, at the Cross. The very name of the Father carries the burden of the Son, once again, written into His Word from the very beginning of creation. Perhaps that explains why the chief priests were so upset with the inscription that Pontus Pilate had written, for in phonetic Hebrew it would read: Y-eshua H-anotzri V-emelech H-ayehudim—YHVH![30]

As I have stated, early on in my study, I was greatly intrigued by the meaning of the word ***nazah*** translated "sprinkle" in the KJV bible. Found in context here:

> Isaiah 52:13 "Behold, my servant shall deal prudently, he shall be exalted and extolled, and be very high. As many were astonied at thee; his visage was so marred more than any man, and his form more than the sons of men: So shall he *sprinkle* many nations; the kings shall shut their mouths at him: for *that* which had not been told them shall they see; and *that* which they had not heard shall they consider." (Emphasis added)

In fact, it could be argued that the word *nazah* has kept me investigating for most of these years. Let's re-visit the Hebrew meanings associated with it: Nâzâh, נָזָה *naw-zaw'* A primitive root; to *spirt*, that is, *besprinkle* (especially in expiation): - sprinkle. BDB Definition: 1) to spurt, spatter, sprinkle 1a) (Qal) to spurt, spatter 1b) (Hiphil) to cause to spurt, sprinkle upon 2) to spring, leap 2a) (Hiphil) to cause to leap, startle.

---

30 Arno Lamm and Emile Andre Vanbeckevoort, **Wake Up**, p.235, (Doorn Netherlands, Stichting Het Zoeklicht, Feb. 2017 ISBN-13:9789064512384

The concept that the marred face and body of the servant of Hashem would both sprinkle and startle captured my conviction that more in depth understanding of the Scripture would help unravel the mystery of the Shroud of Turin. The Hebrew pictographs offered an entirely new level of promising research. Most importantly, my own depth of knowledge took a quantum leap when I realized what the ancient Hebrew pictographs had to say.

The word "*nazah*" in Hebrew is: נָזָה

Reading from right to left in Hebrew, according to the ancient pictographic meaning, the result is:

Behold, the heir to the throne, pierced.

The Scriptural cross reference which should be an obvious connection for the *Berean* (one who receives the message eagerly and examines the Scriptures daily, see Acts 17:10–12) is found in the book of the prophet Zechariah:

> Zechariah 12:10 "And I will pour upon the house of David, and upon the inhabitants of Jerusalem, the spirit of grace and of supplications: and *they shall look upon me whom they have pierced*, and they shall mourn for him, as one mourneth for *his* only *son*, and shall be in bitterness for him, as one that is in bitterness for *his* firstborn." (Emphasis added)

However the original Hebrew is even more revealing for there is an untranslated letter combination in the middle of the verse. It actually reads as follows: "…they shall look on me (את) whom they have pierced." Because there are numerous examples of this exact letter combination it behooves us to note a few other examples. The first is found in Genesis 1:1 which actually reads "In the beginning God (את) created the Heavens and the earth." Perhaps that is why ancient rabbis believed that the untranslated "את" pointed to the unspeakable Name of God. Of more importance to this treatise are other examples of the hidden את. For example, in Exodus 12:13 and 12:23 the את precedes the "blood!" So when Yeshua says to John in Revelation 1:8 "I am the Aleph and the Tav," we need to understand the Hebrew expression that is used there. It is actually "אות"-"The leader nailed on the cross." How much more confirmation do we need of the very Hand of the Most High in all of Scripture?[31]

Yeshua, Himself states in Matthew 18:16 "But if he will not hear *thee, then* take with thee one or two more, that in the mouth of two or three witnesses every word may be established." Apostle Paul reiterates that same truth in 2Corinthians 13:1 "This *is* the third *time* I am coming to you. In the mouth of two or three witnesses shall every word be established." In fact, the Torah requires multiple witnesses as noted in the book of Numbers.

> Numbers 35:30 "Whoso killeth any person, the murderer shall be put to death by the mouth of *witnesses*: *but one witness* shall not testify against any person *to cause him* to die." (Emphasis added)

And again in the book of Deuteronomy:

---

31   Arno Lamm and Emile Andre Vanbeckevoort, **Wake Up**, pp.56, 58, 232-233, (Doorn Netherlands, Stichting Het Zoeklicht, Feb. 2017 ISBN-13:9789064512384

> Deuteronomy 17:6 "At the mouth of *two witnesses,* or *three witnesses,* shall he that is worthy of death be put to death; *but* at the mouth of one witness he shall not be put to death." (Emphasis added)

And again,

> Deuteronomy 19:15 "One witness shall not rise up against a man for any iniquity, *or* for any sin, in any sin that he sinneth: at the mouth of *three witnesses,* shall the matter be established." (Emphasis added)

The point being, when multiple confirmations appear in Scripture, the presumption of truth is "established." The incredible number of references which confirm the piercing of the Messiah should be more than sufficient to dispel any disbelief in the identification of Yeshua as the promised "Lamb of G-d" slain before the foundation of the world. When I first set out to delve into the Scriptures, I had no idea the direction it would take, nor the depth of confirmation I would find. Nevertheless, from my earliest presentation (in or about 2004) that I made about the research path that I was taking, I called it, "White Linen and the Blood of Sprinkling" based solely upon the passage in Isaiah, chapter 52. It wasn't until I was wrapping up the initial chapters that I stumbled upon the ancient Hebrew pictographic significance.

As with any search for authenticity itself, it is not any one thing that makes the case beyond a shadow of any doubt, it is the total package. In order to make a clear decision you must look at all the facts, only then can you reach a validated conclusion. We're ready to take a look at the "Big Picture" now.

SEEING THE "BIG PICTURE"

2 Peter 1:16–21 "For we have not followed cunningly devised fables, when we made known unto you the power and coming of our Lord Jesus Christ, but were eyewitnesses of his majesty. For he received from God the Father honor and glory, when there came such a voice to him from the excellent glory, this is my beloved Son, in whom I am well pleased. And this voice which came from heaven we heard, when we were with him in the holy mount. We have also a more sure word of prophecy; whereunto ye do well that ye take heed, as unto a light that shineth in a dark place, until the day dawn, and the day star arise in your hearts: Knowing this first, that no prophecy of the scripture is of any private interpretation. For the prophecy came not in old time

by the will of man: but holy men of God spake *as they were moved by the Holy Ghost."*

T he story is told of the six blind men who attempt to describe an elephant. After each man examines only one part of the animal, they give six different opinions as to how to describe the elephant. None of them correctly describe the elephant, and even taken together their separate descriptions also fail miserably to provide the "big picture." Sindonology (the science of the study of the Shroud of Turin) has been hampered by a similar issue for far too long. Proponents and opponents alike often base their conclusions on woefully incomplete information.

The case for authenticity becomes overwhelming when all the evidence is considered together. In fact, we can now update the conclusion of STURP in 1981: "We can conclude for now that the Shroud image is that of a real human form of a scourged, crucified man. It is **NOT** the product of an artist. The bloodstains are composed of hemoglobin and also give a positive test for serum albumin. The image is an ongoing mystery and until further chemical studies are made, perhaps by this group of scientists, or perhaps by some scientists in the future, the problem remains unsolved."[32]With the intervening thirty-five years of on-going research the odds are astronomically in favor of only one conclusion the Shroud of Turin **IS** the authentic burial garment of Yeshua of Nazareth. As such, this cloth **IS** the "most awesome and instructive relic" of faith the world has ever seen.

Sadly, to a certain extent, we live in what the Bible describes as "perilous times," and Peter, Paul, and Jude all attest to that fact. The following Scriptures describe an era in which self-indulgence, scoffing, twisting the Scriptures and a denial by Man

32   STURP, Summary, 1981

of the evidence, even for the existence of G-D, would bring about more and more depravity.

2Peter 3:1–4 "This second epistle, beloved, I now write unto you; in *both* which I stir up your pure minds by way of remembrance: that ye may be mindful of the words which were spoken before by the holy prophets, and of the commandment of us the apostles of the Lord and Saviour: knowing this first, that there shall come in the last days scoffers, walking after their own lusts, and saying, Where is the promise of his coming? For since the fathers fell asleep, all things continue as *they were* from the beginning of the creation."

2Peter 3:15–18 "Bear in mind that the patience of our Lord means salvation—just as our dearly loved brother Paul also wrote to you with the wisdom given to him. He speaks about these matters in all of his letter. Some things in them are hard to understand, which the ignorant and unstable twist (as they do with the rest of the Scriptures)—to their own destruction. Since you already know all this, loved ones, be on your guard so that you are not led astray by the error of the lawless and lose your sure footing. Instead, keep growing in the grace and knowledge of our Lord and Savior Yeshua the Messiah. To Him be the glory both now and to the day of eternity! Amen." TLV

2Timothy 3:1–4 "This know also, that in the last days perilous times shall come. For men shall be lovers of their own selves, covetous, boasters, proud, blasphemers, disobedient to parents, unthankful, unholy, without natural affection, trucebreakers, false accusers, incontinent, fierce, despisers of those that are good, traitors, heady, high minded, lovers of pleasures more than lovers of God;"

2Timothy 3:13 "But evil men and seducers shall wax worse and worse, deceiving, and being deceived."

Romans 1:18–22 "For the wrath of God is revealed from heaven against all ungodliness and unrighteousness of men, who hold the truth in unrighteousness; because that which may be known of God is manifest in them; for God hath shewed *it* unto them. For the invisible things of him from the creation of the world are clearly seen, being understood by the things that are made, *even* his eternal power and Godhead; so that they are without excuse: because that, when they knew God, they glorified *him* not as God, neither were thankful; but became vain in their imaginations, and their foolish heart was darkened. Professing themselves to be wise, they became fools."

2Thessalonians 2:10–12 "And with all deceivableness of unrighteousness in them that perish; because they received not the love of the truth, that they might be saved. And for this cause God shall send them strong delusion, that they should believe a lie: That they all might be damned who believed not the truth, but had pleasure in unrighteousness."

Jude 1:3–5 "Loved ones, though very eager to write to you about our common salvation, I felt it necessary to write to you urging you to continue to contend for the faith that was once for all handed down to the kedoshim. For certain people have secretly slipped in—those who from long ago have been marked out for this judgment. They are ungodly people, who pervert the grace of our God into indecency and deny our only Master and Lord, Yeshua the Messiah. Now I wish to remind you—though you have come to know all things—that the Lord, once having saved a people out of the land of Egypt, afterward destroyed those who did not believe." TLV

Jude 1:11–16 "Woe to them! For they went the way of Cain; they were consumed for pay in Balaam's error; and in Korah's rebellion they have been destroyed. These people are hidden rocky reefs at your love feasts—shamelessly feasting with you, tending only to themselves. They are waterless clouds, carried along by winds; fruitless trees in late autumn, doubly dead, uprooted; wild waves of the sea, foaming up their own shame; wandering stars, for whom the gloom of utter darkness has been reserved forever. It was also about these people that Enoch, the seventh generation from Adam, prophesied, saying, "Behold, the Lord came with myriads of His kedoshim, to execute judgment against all. He will convict all the ungodly for all their ungodly deeds that they have done in an ungodly way, and for all of the harsh things ungodly sinners have spoken against Him." These are bellyaching grumblers, following after their own desires. Their mouth speaks grandiose things, showing favoritism for the sake of gain." TLV

Personally, by the time I completed college, the faith that was instilled in me as a child was barely an ember. I had more questions than I had answers to the great mysteries of life. When my instructor pilot and a former roommate from the Air Force Academy began to share with me their faith in Yeshua as Messiah, that ember was fanned into a flame that continues to burn after 47 years. In one of the strangest (G-d) incidences of my early walk as a new believer, we were discussing the passion and death of Yeshua during a Bible study. Suddenly, I remembered a detailed presentation and slide show about the Shroud from a Catholic retreat years before. With excitement I began to share what I remembered and that was met with such disdain and hostility that I was shocked. The study leader reminded me of the unsavory history of selling fake relics and indulgences that was a well-known facet of medieval Catholicism. Somewhat "licking my wounds" I said as best I recall, "Well *if* what I remember is true, Christians should be shouting about *this* relic and not trying to sweep it under the rug!" Over the years I have jokingly opined that an angel must have heard me say that and reported it to the Lord, "Well, we have someone who will tell the story of the Shroud." What is no joke, however, is the path that took me to my involvement with the actual research effort and what has surely become a lifetime avocation.

As the story goes, my great-grandmother, who was an evangelist before women were widely accepted in ministry, told my grandmother to raise my mother as a Catholic. She never changed her own Protestant evangelical faith, nor the faith of any other family members as far as I know. The Catholic education that I received enabled me to excel academically and eventually receive an appointment to the United States Air Force Academy (USAFA); the most important stepping stone in my life-long dream to become a pilot.

Following pilot training, I served as a B-52 pilot on three consecutive tours in Vietnam, where in December of 1972, I experienced a miraculous escape from a surface-to-air missile that literally was locked onto my aircraft. Following that mission, I thanked the Lord in prayer and promised to do whatever HE wanted me to do in life. Two years later I was on directed duty to earn a Master's degree pursuant to returning to the USAFA faculty to teach. Two years after that I was in a car pool with three other USAFA instructors, and a discussion of faith led to the formation of the Shroud of Turin Research Project. Forty years later, I am writing my fifth book on the subject. (On the first, I was only a contributor and editor.) My goal in each book has been to present *all* the facts so that the reader can reach an educated decision and not merely accept the sound bites and spin doctoring so prevalent in our day and age. Coincidentally, of the forty original researchers who journeyed to Turin in 1978, to date I am the only one who has attempted to author comprehensive books on the Shroud, which brings us to this current tome.

For over forty years now, I have seen otherwise "*educated*" people virtually twist themselves into mental pretzels to avoid the logical conclusions that are presented when all of the facts concerning the Shroud are known. At times the self-deception is unbelievable. So, let us first review the facts as they are known.

When "*The Shroud and the Controversy*" was published twenty-six years ago, the following facts were already confirmed and theories of image-formation were already well established, tested and peer-reviewed.

From The Shroud and the Controversy
APPENDIX B
Comparison of Image-Formation Theories with Image Characteristics

THEORIES						
	*Paint, Dye or Powder	*Direct Contact	*Vapor	*Direct Contact and Vapor	*Unknown Energy Source	German-Pellicori Direct Contact + Unknown Variable
CHARACTERISTICS:						
Superficial	No	No	No	No	Yes	Possible
Detailed	No	No	No	Possible	Possible	No
Thermally Stable	No	Possible	No	Possible	Yes	Yes
Pigment	No	Possible	Yes	Yes	Yes	Yes
3-D	No	No	No	No	Yes	Possible **
Negative	Yes	Possible	Possible	Possible	Yes	Yes
Directionless	Possible	Possible	Yes	Yes	Yes	Yes
Chemically Stable	Possible	Possible	No	No	Yes	Possible
Water Stable	Possible	Possible	No	No	Yes	Yes
UV Image						
Fluorescence	-	-	-	-	No	No

*	**Discounted by Scientists**
**	**Disagreement among Scientists**

Facts: a) an actual burial garment of a man crucified exactly like Christ

         b) image characteristics:

1) superficial
2) photographically negative
3) encoded with 3-Dimensional information
4) composed of degraded/dehydrated cellulous fibers
5) non-directional
6) detailed: enough for a virtual autopsy
7) thermally stable
8) chemically stable
9) water stable
10) infrared positive
11) sepia toned
12) blood prevents image formation (it was there first)
13) blood is human
14) similar color spectrum to a scorch
15) NEVER successfully duplicated
16) no pigment, powders or dyes
17) Scripturally accurate

APPENDIX C

Summary of Critiques of Alternative Image-Formation Hypotheses

After much research on the Shroud of Turin, we have concluded that the most probable theory is that the image of the cloth was formed by some kind of scorching process. However, other hypotheses have been suggested to explain how the image was formed, and many of them have appeared in the popular press. For documentation and further explanation, see Chapter 8

(The Shroud and the Controversy) and *Verdict on the Shroud*, pp. 191–197.

I. **Fraud Hypotheses: These Theories Maintain that the Shroud Was Created by One of Several Forms of Fakery.**

   A. General theories of fraud which indicate that the image was created by the application of paint, dye, powder, or other foreign substance to the Shroud

      1. Microchemical analyses revealed no pigments, stains, powders, dyes, or painting media on the Shroud. Several such tests were performed, including photoreflectance and ultraviolet fluorescence, all agreeing that no fakery is involved. In particular, X-ray fluorescence was considered the major test for detecting such fraud, and it revealed no foreign substance in the image area which could account for the image itself.

      2. Fraud is refuted by the Shroud's 3-D characteristics.

      3. Fakery is disproven by the superficial nature of the image.

      4. There are no plateaus or saturation points on the Shroud image, as would be expected with applications of pigment, dye, etc.

      5. The non-directionality of the image rules out brush strokes or other directional application of a foreign substance.

      6. No capillary flow appears on the Shroud, which further rules out any liquid movement on the cloth.

7. The 1532 fire would have caused chemical changes in organic pigments, but no such changes are visible on the Shroud.

8. The water applied to the Shroud after the 1532 fire would also have caused chemical changes in many pigments, but none can be observed on the Shroud image.

9. The nontraditional body image (pierced wrists, a cap of thorns, and possibly nude body) also militates against fraud.

B. Walter McCrone: Iron oxide was used to touch up or to create the Shroud image

1. McCrone must account for refutations IA: 1–9 above, which invalidate his hypothesis.

2. The scientists specifically checked McCrone's thesis with highly sensitive microchemical tests and found that Fe_2O_2 does not account for the Shroud image.

3. Submicron-size Fe_2O_2 has been available only within the last two hundred years, making its use in medieval times highly problematical.

4. McCrone's observations have not been verified by independent testing.

C. Joe Nickell: Various ideas that ink or powder application produced the Shroud image (see Bibliography)

1. Refutations IA 1–9 above invalidate Nickell's thesis.

2. Nickell's photographs were specifically tested and failed the three-dimensional VP-8 analysis, thus indicating high probability that his methods did not create the true 3-D image on the Shroud.

3. Such a method would probably involve image saturation, which would probably involve image saturation, which would invalidate it.

4. Nickell's experiment did not recreate the resolution of the Shrod image.

5. Nickell's "squeeze" method apparently is not historically verified as a known technique used before the nineteenth century.

D. "Acid Painting:" Addition of an acid or other chemical to cloth to produce an image

1. Refutations IA 1–9 above also invalidate this thesis.

2. Experiments revealed that acid painting is not superficial. That is, the chemical does not remain only on the surface of the material.

3. Testing also revealed that densities from such techniques differ from densities in the Shroud image.

4. Acid-painting involves an additional consideration in that if the acid is not neutralized, it will destroy the cloth.

II. **Vaporgraph Theories: These Theories Assert That the Shroud Image Was Created by the Diffusion of Gases Upward onto the Burial Cloth from Such Sources as Sweat, Ammonia, Blood, and Burial Spices.**

A. Vaporgraphs cannot account for the 3-D nature of the Shroud image.

B. The superficial Shroud image refutes vaporgraphic theories because such gases permeate the cloth and are not superficial.

C. There are no plateaus or saturation in the image, as would happen with vapor stains.

D. Vaporgraphs don't yield a clear image like that on the Shroud. Since vapor does not travel upward in straight or parallel lines, but diffuses in the air, vapor images are comparatively unclear.

E. No gaseous diffusion or capillary flow can be observed on the Shroud's image fibrils. These should be present in a vaporgraph.

F. Vaporgraphic images do not preserve the shading found in the Shroud image.

G. More ammonia is needed to create a vaporgraph than would probably be available on a dead body.

H. No foreign material is found on the Shroud image from such chemical reactions.

I. Few of these chemicals from or on the body are thermally stable, as is the Shroud image.

J. Many of these chemicals are active in water, but the Shroud image is stable in water.

K. Vaporgraphic theories cannot account for the transfer of the images of hair or coins.

III. Contact Theories: These Hypotheses Assert That the Shroud Image Is from Either Natural Contact with a Body or Contact Due to Fakery.

A. General objections to all contact theories, natural or fake:

1. Contact images would not be 3-D, thereby eliminating them as viable hypotheses.

2. The superficial nature of the image is also a major critique of contact theories.

3. The absence of plateaus or saturation in the Shroud image also mitigates against contact.

4. A contact image would rely on pressure. The fact that the Shroud reveals virtually the same density on the frontal and dorsal images indicates a pressure-independent image formation.

5. That there are no chemicals on the Shroud is an important indicator that mitigates against any chemical transfer by contact.

6. The shading in the Shroud image probably eliminates contact.

7. The 1532 fire militates against the Shroud being formed by contact with natural organic materials.

8. Many chemicals are water active, but the Shroud image is not.

9. Resolution is still very difficult to explain by contact.

10. The question of whether contact theories can properly explain the transfer of the hari or the coins should also be considered.

B. Direct contact-latent image hypothesis: Attributes the Shroud image to natural contact with a body, transferring chemicals and causing the image over a period of time

1. This hypothesis is still shown to be untenable by refutations IIIA: 1–10 above, which disprove it, as some specific examples will show.

2. The latent image form of direct contact still cannot account for the 3-D image. For instance, not all areas of the body (the face, for example) were contacted by the cloth, yet even these areas are

found on the Shroud image. To use our example, there are no face "drop outs" in the Shroud image. Therefore, this contact theory cannot adequately explain the image.

3. Superficiality is still a major problem for this method as well since the Shroud image does not generally follow dips in the threads.

4. The Shroud image lacks saturation points or plateaus, which severely limits the time dependence of this model.

5. Whereas the Shroud image is pressure independent, this contact hypothesis would be pressure dependent, as with the weight of the body on the dorsal image and the cloth on the frontal image being responsible for the image. This is a very serious obstacle for this model.

6. There are no traces on the Shroud of sensitizing chemicals from any such contact procedures.

7. It would seem that this hypothesis also cannot explain the transfer of the hair in the Shroud image.

8. Some question the experimental method used to represent accelerated aging.

9. If such a reaction can normally occur between a dead body and a burial cloth, why don't more burial garments also have such an image? Many grave clothes exist, but the Shroud image is unique. No others are known to have a body image at all.

C. The "hot statue" and "hot flat-plate" theories: A statue or flat-plate image of a man was heated and a cloth laid across it, producing a contact or near-contact scorch

1. Many of the objections (IIIA: 1–10) above still apply to these theories and thereby render them untenable.

2. The 1532 fire is very helpful here in that it did produce a contact scorch in a variety of densities. However, ultraviolet fluorescence photographs showed that these scorched areas do fluoresce while the body image does not, thereby revealing that they are different. There is also a color difference between the two types of fibrils.

3. Experiments have shown that hot statue or hot place-plate images are not superficial, thus invalidating these methods.

4. A hot statue or hot flat-plate is distorted. The Shroud image distinctly lacks distortion.

5. Experiments revealed that such a hot statue or hot flat-plate scorch would not produce the shading found on the Shroud.

6. A hot statue or hot flat-plate forgery would be very difficult to create without burning the cloth beyond recognition of any image.

7. The resolution of the Shroud image is another difficult issue for a hot statue or hot flat-plate.[33]

---

33   Kenneth Stevenson & Gary Habermas, **The Shroud and the Controversy**, (Tenn., Thomas Nelson, 1990) pp. 214–225

At this point, the picture forming is that of an actual burial garment of a Shephardic Jewish man between 30–35 years of age, who has been crucified exactly as Yeshua was, including those "singular" details which historically have *only* been associated with Him. Furthermore, the image formation process remains a mystery which has defied *every* attempt at reproduction, including the use of space-age technology. While man-made images have duplicated *some* of the known characteristics of the Shroud, there is no technique that has captured all of the unique characteristics of this enigmatic cloth. Furthermore, the cloth clearly had its origins, not in Europe, but rather in the Middle East, not only is its manufacture consistent with that fact, but it is also confirmed with pollens and floral evidence from Jerusalem and Turkey.[34]

---

34 Stevenson & Habermas, **Controversy**, p.77

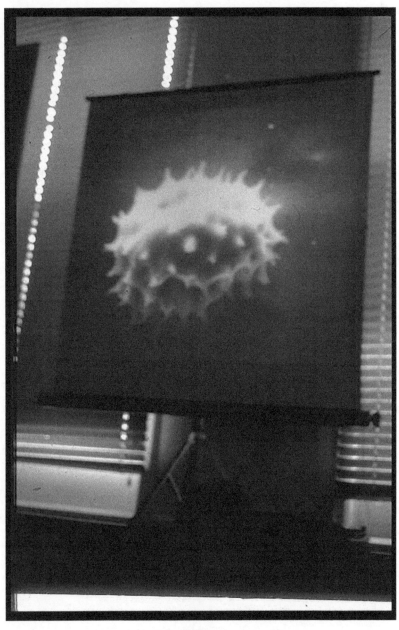

Pollen

Hints of the knowledge of its existence and incredible imagery are turning up in extra-biblical sources and liturgy as well. In depth analysis of the Scriptures themselves give an ever broadening look into just how well the Shroud of Turin follows the Biblical pattern, promise and purpose of Hashem's redemption plan of the Lamb slain before the foundation of the world.

Recently, while working on this book, I wanted to create a bullet list of factors to send out to those who might consider hosting my multi-media presentation on the Shroud. What follows is that list in its entirety just as it was sent out:

Twelves Reasons to Prayerfully Consider Hosting the Presentation of Dr. Kenneth E. Stevenson on the Shroud of Turin

1. One of the 40 scientists from the top laboratories and institutions who actually participated in an historic six 24 hour a day hands on testing of the Shroud of Turin as the original spokesman and editor for that research, Dr. Kenneth Stevenson has authored comprehensive books on the subject which have impacted lives for the Gospel around the world.

2. Contrary to popular belief, the C-14 testing did not prove the Shroud was medieval. Peer-reviewed scientific re-testing has proven the piece of cloth dated was in fact NOT linen at all, but rather a cotton patch that was woven into the Shroud following the fire that severely damaged the cloth in 1532.

3. The Shroud matches Jewish burial custom according to the Code of Law: Book of Mourning, but not "traditional" beliefs concerning Christ's burial. "Then took they the body of Jesus, and wound it in linen clothes with the spices, as the manner of the Jews is to bury" (John 19:40).

4. There is much Scriptural and liturgical evidence that points to the Shroud.

5. The 3-Dimensional characteristic of the image on the Shroud is absolutely unique, no man made effort has ever been able to accurately recreate this characteristic.

6. The man in the Shroud, anthropologically speaking, is a Shephardic Jew estimated at 30–35 years of age whose death and burial as recorded in this image is identical to that of Yeshua Ha Nazaret. There is enough detail for a virtual autopsy to be performed.

7. The Shroud is an actual burial garment and to date no one has ever been able to recreate ALL of the known characteristics of the Shroud, even with all of our modern technology at hand.

8. The Shroud fulfills most of the major prophecies cited by author Peter Stoner in calculating the odds that anyone else in history could be the Messiah at 1×10^{17}.

9. The Shroud could hold the prophetic key to the salvation of the Jews in these last days.

10. The image on the Shroud is the most accurate depiction of the death and burial of Jesus Christ ever found.

11. Modern technology and criminology confirms the Shroud originated in the Middle East and not Europe, and the details that emerge match a historical trail that was not proposed until 1978.

12. Without exception, lives have been changed wherever this lecture is seen.

For almost forty years I have spoken about the Shroud of Turin. At every lecture I make a few things clear: 1) while I believe the Shroud to be genuine, if when I am finished someone still does not, that's fine! 2)the most important things I *did* come to do is to reveal what it cost Yeshua to go to the Cross for the sins of *all* Mankind 3) the Shroud is a real burial garment and not a "forgery" of any kind 4) it contains the most accurate record of death by crucifixion ever seen.

In all that time, *many* have received what Rabbi Paul called "his unspeakable gift," and none to my knowledge have every ended by making the Shroud into an "idol."

> 2Corinthians 9:15 "Thanks *be* unto God for his unspeakable gift."

If by now the reader has considered the significance of G-D's precious gift as revealed on the Shroud, then we should next discuss the significance of seeing G-D *face to face*.

FACE TO FACE

Genesis 32:30 "And Jacob called the name of the place Peniel: *for I have seen God face to face*, and my life is preserved."

In a very strange way, one of the most challenging arguments posed for the Shroud of Turin is the image itself. Notwithstanding all of the unique characteristics of the Shroud: photographic negative, very superficial, encoded with three-dimensional data, no pigments, powders or dyes in its makeup, without equal in art, defying reproduction—it is still an *image*. While those very characteristics compel the most intense scientific inquiry, they also invite rejection from both the iconoclast as well as the Scripture adherent. The most often asked question being: "Why would Hashem, given man's proclivity for idolatry, leave an image for man to find? Much less an image on a burial shroud, which most societies would deem unclean?" Why, indeed.

141

To begin with, we must come to grips with the fact that G-D does not think or reason in the same way that we do. As I pointed out earlier, the prophet Isaiah declares this truth for us:

> Isaiah 55:8–9 "For my thoughts are not your thoughts, neither are you ways my ways, saith the LORD. For *as* the heavens are higher than the earth, so are my ways higher than your ways, and my thoughts than your thoughts."

In Gans Eden, Adam and Eve had direct fellowship with G-D. So much so that they even recognized His voice after the fall, and in context, it must have been normal for Him to walk in the Garden at that time. The logical conclusion, would be that they saw G-D *face to face*.

> Genesis 3:8 "And they heard the voice of the LORD God walking in the garden in the cool of the day."

Furthermore, Hashem tells Solomon, the "wisest" man to walk the earth, that when we fall, unlike Adam and Eve who hid themselves, we are instead to "*seek His face.*" Most significantly, they were to seek His face when they fell.

> 2Chronicles 7:14 "If my people, which are called by my name, shall humble themselves, and pray, and *seek my face*, and turn from their wicked ways; then will I hear from heaven, and will forgive their sin, and will heal their land."

Indeed, seven times in the Torah, we are given examples of "*face to face*" meetings with the Lord G-D.

Genesis 32:30 "And Jacob called the name of the place Peniel: for I have seen God *face to face*, and my life is preserved."

Exodus 33:11 "And the LORD spake unto Moses *face to face*, as a man speaketh unto his friend. And he turned again into the camp: but his servant Joshua, the son of Nun, a young man, departed not out of the tabernacle."

Numbers 14:14 "And they will tell *it* to the inhabitants of the this land: *for* they have heard that thou LORD *art* among this people, that thou LORD art seen *face to face*, and *that* thy cloud standeth over them, and *that* thou goest before them, by day time in a pillar of a cloud, and in a pillar of fire by night."

Deuteronomy 5:4 "The LORD talked with you *face to face* in the mount out of the midst of the fire."

Deuteronomy 34:10 "And there arose not a prophet since in Israel like unto Moses, whom the LORD knew *face to face*."

Judges 6:22 "And when Gideon perceived that he *was* an angel of the LORD, Gideon said, Alas O Lord GOD! For because I have seen an angel of the LORD *face to face*."

Ezekiel 20:35 "And I will bring you into the wilderness of the people, and there will I plead with you *face to face*."

Yet G-D's clear intentions for restoring that Edenic condition do not end there. David, the "sweet psalmist of Israel" records for us the following confirmation:

> Psalm 17:15 "As for me, I will behold *thy face* in righteousness: I shall be satisfied, when I awake, with *thy likeness.*"

Job, for his part, makes the point that seeing the *face of G-d* will be his portion in the resurrection *because* of the "kinsman redeemer." Yeshua, by His death, burial and resurrection *is* the Redeemer!

> Job 19:25–27 "For I know *that my redeemer liveth*, and *that* he shall stand at the latter *day* upon the earth: And *though* after my skin *worms* destroy this *body, yet in my flesh shall I see God*: Whom I shall see for myself, and *mine eyes shall behold*, and not another; *though* my reins be consumed within me." (Emphasis added)

Furthermore, David and Solomon are not the only ones to report that we are specifically to "*seek His face*" when we have fallen from His grace! Thy prophet Hosea conveys the exact same truth:

> Hosea 5:15 "I will go *and* return to my place, till they acknowledge their offence, and *seek my face*: in their affliction they will seek me early."

In point of fact, there are numerous instances in Scripture that make it plain the Lord would have a "*face to face* relationship with all HIS creation. Yet the question we still want to resolve is *would* Hashem use an image which could lead to idolatry in the sinful heart of mankind? Which reminds us of a pivotal event that took place soon after Israel was delivered from Egypt.

The Bronze Serpent

Numbers 21:4–9 "And they journeyed from mount Hor by the way of the Red sea, to compass the land of Edom: and the soul of the people was much discouraged because of the way. And the people spake against God, and against Moses, Wherefore have ye brought us up out of Egypt to die in the wilderness? For *there is* no bread, neither *is there any* water; and our soul loatheth this light bread. And the LORD sent fiery serpents among the people, and they bit the people; and much people of Israel died. Therefore the people came to Moses, and said, we have sinned, for we have spoken against the LORD, and against thee; pray unto the LORD, that he take away the serpents from us. And Moses prayed for the people. And the LORD said unto Moses, Make thee a fiery serpent, and set it upon a pole: and it shall come to pass, that every one that is bitten, when he looketh upon it, shall live. And Moses made a serpent of brass, and put it upon a pole, and it came to pass, that if a serpent had bitten any man, when he beheld the serpent of brass, he lived."

The sin of the people was healed by "looking upon the serpent on a pole," but in later years the thing became an idol to Israel. Why then would Yeshua state clearly to Nicodemus, a ruler in the synagogue, that He must be treated like the serpent on the pole? The serpent brought sin to the human race and therefore the serpent is synonymous with sin. Looking at the serpent on the pole was a step of faith because there is no logical efficacy or natural healing to be found by merely "looking" at a serpent on a pole. But Yeshua declared he would be lifted up like that serpent.

> John 3:14 "And as Moses lifted up the serpent in the wilderness, even so must the Son of man be lifted up:"

As Rabbi Paul will explain to the saints at Corinth and Galatia, Yeshua became synonymous with sin in order to redeem us all from the penalty of sin which is death (Romans 6:23).

> 2Corinthians 5:21 "For he hath made him *to be* sin for us, who knew no sin; that we might be made the righteousness of God in him."

> Galatians 3:13 "Messiah liberated us from Torah's curse, having become a curse for us (for it is written, "Cursed is everyone who hangs on a tree") TLV

> Colossians 2:12–15 "You were buried along with Him in immersion, through which you also were raised with Him by trusting in the working of God, who raised Him from the dead. When you were dead in your sins and the uncircumcision of your flesh, God made you alive together with Him when He pardoned us all our transgressions. He wiped out the handwritten record of debts with the decrees against us, which was hostile to us. He took it away by nailing it to the cross. After disarming the principalities and powers, He made a public spectacle of them, triumphing over them in the cross."

The spotless Lamb became the sacrifice which all must look upon in faith. Later in His earthly ministry Yeshua gives the explanation that makes it all so clear *to them that believe.*

> John 12:32–40 "And as I am lifted up from the earth, I will draw all to Myself. He said this to show the kind of death He was about to die. The crowd answered Him, "We've heard from Scripture that the Messiah remains forever. How can You say, 'The Son of Man must be lifted up?' Who is this Son of Man?" Therefore Yeshua said to them, "The light is with you for a little longer. Walk while you have the light, so that the darkness will not overtake you. The one who walks in darkness doesn't know where he is going. While you have the light, believe in the light so that you may become sons of light." Yeshua spoke these things, then left and hid Himself from them. But even though He had performed so many signs before them, they weren't trusting in Him. This was to fulfill the word of Isaiah the prophet, who said, "Adonai, who has believed out report? To whom has the arm of Adonai been revealed?" (Isaiah 53:1) For this reason they could not believe, for Isaiah also said, "He *has blinded their eyes and hardened their hearts,* so they might not see with *their eyes* nor understand with their hearts and turn back, and I would heal them. (Jeremiah 5:21; Ezekiel 12:2)." TLV (Emphasis added)

Now also the words of Rabbi Paul come back to us once again in confirmation:

1Corinthians 13:12 "For *now we see through a glass, darkly*, but then *face to face*: now I know in part; but then shall I know even as also I am known."

2Corinthians 3:18 "But *we all, with unveiled face beholding as in a mirror the glory of the Lord*, are being transformed *into the same image* from glory to glory—just as from the Lord, who is the Spirit."

2Corinthians 4:6 "For God, who said, "Let light shine out of darkness," is the One who has shone in our hearts, to give *the light of the knowledge of the glory of God in the face of Messiah*." TLV (Emphasis added)

Here, intrinsically, is found the answer to the dilemma of idolatry. If Yeshua *is* in fact the Messiah as He claims to be, and as innumerable faithful, both Jew and Gentile, have proclaimed, then there is indeed a direct connection between the prophetic Word of G-D and this burial linen. Furthermore, Yeshua Himself equated the same to the "serpent on the pole."

Some years ago when my first book "*Verdict on the Shroud*" hit the stands, the late Dr. D. James Kennedy, Pastor of Coral Ridge in Florida, used it to teach a powerful message that he entitled "Save the Wrappings." Not too long thereafter I had the honor to meet him and thank him personally that he had chosen my book out of the many on the Shroud of Turin. His sermon confirmed in my heart what I truly believed: that G-D had an incredible purpose to save the Shroud, as well as to hide it for the proper time. Next, we will answer the question, "Why now?"

FOR SUCH
A TIME AS THIS

Ecclesiastes 3:1 "To every *thing there is* a season, and *a time to every purpose* under the heaven."

Esther 4:14 "For if thou altogether holdest thy peace at this time, then shall there enlargement and deliverance arise to the Jews from another place; but thou and thy father's house shall be destroyed: and who knoweth whether thou art come to the kingdom *for such a time as this?"*

Speaking from a Biblical perspective, G-D has a time and purpose for everything and everyone according to HIS, "… *good, and acceptable, and perfect, will…*" (Romans 12:2).

Ecclesiastes 3:11 *"He hath made every thing beautiful in his time: also he hath set the world in their heart, so that no man can find out the work that God maketh from the beginning to the end."* (Emphasis added)

It is my heart felt conviction that the Shroud of Turin has such a season, time and purpose that Hashem ordained from *everlasting*: a purpose whose time has come!

Everlasting: עולם ôlâm, *o-lawm'*, from H5956; properly *concealed*, that is, the *vanishing* point; generally time *out of mind* (past or future), that is (practically) *eternity*; frequentative adverbially (especially with prepositional prefix) *always*: - always (-s), ancient (time), any more, continuance, eternal, (for, [n-]) ever (-lasting, -more, of old), lasting, long (time), (of) old (time), perpetual, at any time, (beginning of the) world (+ without end).

In understanding that *time and purpose* for the Shroud, let us revisit the words of Rabbi Paul.

Romans 11:25–29 "For I would not, brethren, that ye should be ignorant of this mystery, lest ye should be wise in your own conceits; *that blindness in part is happened to Israel, until the fullness of the Gentiles be come in." And so all Israel shall be saved:* as it is written, there shall come out of Sion the Deliverer, and shall turn away ungodliness from Jacob: For this *is* my covenant unto them, when I shall take away their sins. As concerning the gospel, *they are* enemies for your sakes: but as touching the election, *they are* beloved for the fathers' sakes. *For the gifts and calling of God are without repentance."* (Emphasis added)

According to the Word of Yeshua Himself, we are living in that time! First of all, Israel became a nation again in fulfillment of the prophetic word of Isaiah.

> Isaiah 66:8 "Who hath heard such a thing? Who hath seen such things? Shall the earth be made to bring forth in one day? *Or* shall a nation be born at once? For as soon as Zion travailed, she brought forth her children."

On May 14, 1948 Israel became the national homeland for the Jewish people after having been scattered around the globe. The "*fig tree*" in Scripture is symbolic of Israel, and Yeshua said the "rebirth" of the fig tree would be a sign of the end times.

> Matthew 24:32–33 "Now learn a parable of the fig tree; When his branch is yet tender, and putteth forth leaves, ye know that summer *is* nigh: So likewise ye, when ye shall see all these things, know that it is near, *even* at the doors."

Furthermore, in words strikingly similar to Rabbi Paul, Yeshua tells His disciples concerning those days:

> Luke 21:24 "And they shall fall by the edge of the sword, and shall be led away captive into all nations: and *Jerusalem shall be trodden down of the Gentiles, until the times of the Gentiles be fulfilled.*" (Emphasis added)

On June 7, 1967, during the Six-Day War, Jerusalem was retaken for the first time in nearly two thousand years. The reactions of two key figures who were there on that day are particularly worth noting. "We have returned to all that is holy in our land.

We have returned never to be departed from it again." Defense Minister Moishe Dayan, upon reaching the Western Wall.[35] "I felt truly shaken and stood there murmuring a prayer for peace. Motta Gur's paratroopers were struggling to reach the wall and touch it. We stood among a tangle of rugged, battle-weary men who were unable to believe their eyes or restrain their emotions. Their eyes were moist with tears, their speech incoherent. The overwhelming desire was to cling to the wall, to hold on to that great monument as long as possible." Chief of Staff Yitzchak Rabin.[36]

In the very same context, in Luke's Gospel, there is a startling confirmation of just how pivotal that time is on Hashem's time-table.

> Luke 21:28 "And when these things begin to come to pass, then look up, and lift up your heads; for your redemption draweth nigh."

> Luke 21: 31–33 "So likewise ye, _when ye see these things come to pass_, know ye that the kingdom of God _is nigh at hand_. Verily I say unto you, _this generation shall not pass away till all be fulfilled_. Heaven and earth shall pass away: but my words shall not pass away." (Emphasis added)

The generation that not only saw these things but was used of G-D to bring them to pass is quickly passing away and two promises are being fulfilled before our eyes. The Jewish people are accepting Messiah Yeshua in unprecedented numbers. Furthermore, all of the things Yeshua mentioned concerning His

---

35   Moishe Dayan, http://www.sixdaywar.org/content/ReunificationJerusalem.asp

36   Yitzchak Rabin: IBID

soon return are taking place almost daily. Now, let's again look at the words of Rabbi Paul in their full context.

> Romans 11:7–10 "What then? Israel hath not obtained that which he seeketh for; *but the election hath obtained it, and the rest were blinded* (according as it is written, God hath given them the spirit of slumber, *eyes that they should not see, and ears that they should not hear;) unto this day.* And David saith, *let their table be made a snare, and a trap, and a stumblingblock,* and a recompense unto them: *let their eyes be darkened, that they may not see,* and bow down their back always." (Emphasis added)

Once again, a fulfillment of a prophetic word of Isaiah:

> Isaiah 29:10 "For the LORD hath poured out upon you the spirit of deep sleep, and hath closed your eyes: the prophets and your rulers, the seers that he covered."

And again in the book of Romans:

> Romans 11:11–17 "I say then, have they stumbled that they should fall? God forbid: but *rather through their fall salvation is come unto the Gentiles, for to provoke them to jealousy.* Now if the fall of them *be* riches of the world, and the diminishing of them the riches of the Gentiles; how much more their fullness? For *if the casting away of them be the reconciling of the world, what shall the receiving of them be, but life from the dead?* For if the firstfruit *be* holy, the lump *is* also *holy:* and if the root *be* holy, so *are* the branches. And if some of the branches be broken off, and thou, being a wild olive

tree, wert graffed in among them, and with them partakes of the root and fatness of the olive tree?"

The Mystery of Israel's Salvation

Romans 11:25–26 "For I would not, brethren, that ye should be ignorant of this mystery, lest ye should be wise in your own conceits; that *blindness in part is happened to Israel, until the fullness of the Gentiles be come in, And so all Israel shall be saved*: as it is written, there shall come out of Sion the Deliverer, and shall turn away ungodliness from Jacob:" (Emphasis added)

Hashem allowed "blindness" to happen to Israel in order that the Gentiles might also partake of the mercies of G-D and thereby fulfill the three-fold promise made to Abraham, the "Father of faith."

Genesis 22:18 "And *in thy seed shall all the nations of the earth be blessed*; because thou hast obeyed my voice."

Genesis 26:3–5 "Sojourn in this land, and I will be with thee, and will bless thee; for unto thee, and unto thy seed, I will give all these countries, and I *will perform the oath which I sware unto Abraham thy father*; and I will make thy seed to multiply as the stars of heaven, and will give unto thy seed all these countries; and *in thy seed shall all the nations of the earth be blessed*; because *that Abraham obeyed my voice*, and kept my charge, my commandments, my statutes, and my laws." (Emphasis added)

Genesis 28:13–14 "And, behold, the LORD stood above it, and said, *I am the LORD God of Abraham thy father, and the God of Isaac.* And thy seed shall be as the dust of the earth, and thou shalt spread abroad to the west, and to the east, and to the north, and to the south: and in thee and *in thy seed shall all the families of the earth be blessed.*"

There is also another prophecy to take note of in the context of Rabbi Paul's remarks, which also conforms to eschatology.

Romans 11:15 "For if the casting away of them *be* the reconciling of the world, *what shall the receiving of them be, but life from the dead?*" (Emphasis added)

Paul here, in my opinion, refers clearly to what is called in Scripture the "*first resurrection.*" In order to understand the significance of that fact, let us review some of the connected Scriptures.

1Corinthians 15:19–24 "If we have hoped in Messiah in this life alone, we are to be pitied more than all people. But now Messiah has been raised from the dead, the firstfruits of those who have fallen asleep. For since death came through a man, the resurrection of the dead also has come through a Man. For as in Adam all die, so also in Messiah will all be made alive. But each in its own order: Messiah the firstfruits; then, at His coming, those who belong to Messiah; then the end, when He hands over the kingdom to God the Father after He has destroyed all rule and all authority and power. For He must reign until He has put all His enemies under His feet." TLV

1 Thessalonians 4:15–16 "For this we tell you, by the word of the Lord, that we who are alive and remain until the coming of the Lord shall in no way precede those who are asleep. For the Lord Himself shall come down from heaven with a commanding shout, with the voice of the archangel and with the blast of God's shofar, and the dead in Messiah shall rise first." TLV

Revelation 20:2–7 "He seized the dragon—the ancient serpent, who is the devil and Satan—and bound him for *a thousand years*. He also threw him into the abyss and locked and sealed it over him, so that he would not deceive the nations any longer, until the thousand years were completed. After these things, he must be released for a short while. Then I saw thrones, and people sat upon them—those to whom authority to judge was given. And I saw the souls of those who had been beheaded because of their testimony for Yeshua and because of the word of God. They had not worshipped the beast or his image, nor had they received his mark on their forehead or on their hand. And they came to life and reigned with the Messiah for *a thousand years*. The rest of the dead did not come to life until the thousand years were completed. This is the first resurrection. How fortunate and holy is the one who has a share in the first resurrection! Over such the second death has no authority, but they shall be kohanim of God and the Messiah, and they shall reign with Him for *a thousand years*. When *the thousand years* had ended, Satan shall be released from his prison," TLV (Emphasis added)

While declaring the "first resurrection," John mentions the millennial reign of Messiah's reign six times, which calls to mind, first of all, the words of Peter in which he cites Psalms 90, which the Torah attributes to Moishe.

> 2 Peter 3:8 "But don't forget this one thing, loved ones, that with the Lord one day is like a thousand years, and *a thousand years* are like one day." TLV

> Psalms 90:4 "For *a thousand years* in Your sight are like a day just passing by, or like a watch in the night." TLV (Emphasis added)

Rabbi Paul and John the author of Revelations both testify to a coming resurrection of the dead which in turn is connected to the "receiving again of all Israel:" the salvation of the nation of Israel! However, in order to connect *all* the dots we must first review prophecies of Hosea and Zechariah.

> Hosea 5:15 "I will go and return to my place, till they acknowledge their offence, and <u>seek my face</u>: in their affliction they will seek me early."

> Hosea 6:1–3 "*Come, and let us return unto the LORD*: for he hath torn, and he will heal us; he hath smitten, and he will bind us up. After *two days will he revive us: in the third day he will raise us up, and we shall in his sight.* Then shall we know, *if* we follow on to know the LORD: his going forth is prepared as the morning and *he shall come unto us as the rain, as the latter and former rain unto the earth.*" (Emphasis added)

Zechariah 12:1–3 "The burden of the word of the LORD for Israel, saith the LORD, which stretcheth forth the heavens, and layeth the foundation of the earth, and formeth the spirit of man within him. *Behold, I will make Jerusalem a cup of trembling* unto all the people round about, when they shall be in the siege both against Judah *and* against Jerusalem. And *in that day will I make Jerusalem a burdensome stone for all people*: all that burden themselves with it shall be cut in pieces, though all the people of the earth be gathered together against it." (Emphasis added)

Zechariah 12:9 "And it shall come to pass *in that day, that* I will seek to destroy all the nations that come against Jerusalem."

Him Whom They Have Pierced

Zechariah 12:10 "And I will pour upon the house of David, and upon the inhabitants of Jerusalem, the spirit of grace and of supplications: and *they shall look upon me whom they have pierced, and they shall mourn for him,* as one mourneth for *his* only *son,* and shall be in bitterness for him, as one that is in bitterness for *his* firstborn." (Emphasis added)

A Baptist Pastor of London, F.B. Meyer, who was born in 1847 and died in 1929, wrote the following concerning this Zechariah passage: "Zechariah 12:1–14 JERUSALEM'S DAY OF MOURNING. *This vision refers to a time yet future, when the Jews shall have returned to their own land, but still in unbelief; and will be assailed by their foes, though in vain,* Zechariah 12: 2–3; Zechariah

<u>12:6</u>. The Lord will defend them, <u>Zechariah 12:7–8</u>. Then the nation will mourn. Their repentance will be *universal*, from the highest to the lowest. Born almost exactly 101 years before Israel was "born again" as a nation, this pastor clearly saw in prophecy the reality that was coming; which was indeed the beginning of the "generation" in which we are now *living*. Furthermore, tiny Israel, a country no larger than the state of New Jersey, immediately became the focal point of hatred by the surrounding Arab nations, and a sectarian civil war between Palestinian Jews and Arabs became a full out Arab-Israeli war the very month that Israel was reborn: May, 1948. To this day, Jerusalem and Israel indeed continue to be a "*burdensome stone for all people.*" Yet, Scripture makes plain that this condition will continue *until* the "*day of the Lord.*" [37]

> Zechariah 14:1–2 "Behold, *the day of the LORD cometh*, and thy spoil shall be divided in the midst of thee. For I will gather all nations against Jerusalem to battle;"

To sum this up and make clear its connection to the Shroud of Turin, here is what I believe the Scriptures indicate to the "Berean" mind: the Jewish people, who did not initially believe in Yeshua as the promised Messiah, were "blinded" in order that the blessing of Abraham would be fulfilled in the nations. When the Romans destroyed the city in 70 C.E., the Chosen people were scattered just as the Tanach foretold. Nearly two thousand years later, the nation is "reborn" in a day and a pure language is restored. IN addition, the new nation is immediately under assault from all sides. But Hosea declared that in the midst of their affliction, G-d's people would seek His face, and after "two days" He would raise them up, and in the "third day" they would

---

37   F.B. Meyer, **E-Sword Commentary**, (London Circa 1900?)

live in His sight. Even the secular and cultic world have long tried
to interpret the significance of the second millennium of modern
times without any success. However, it is in this exact time frame
that we have witnessed the rise of Chosen People Ministries,
(formerly the American Board of Missions to the Jews) Jews for
Jesus, and many other groups, who, when seeking "His Face" have
come to recognize that Yeshua is indeed Messiah.

So then, what is the Shroud of Turin connection here?
How will they be able to "look" upon the one they have pierced
and also "mourn" for Him? The coming of the Messiah should
be if anything a great cause for rejoicing among His people. The
Hebrew word used here for "look" is *nâbat.* נָבַט Strong's H5027
naw-bat' a primitive root; to *scan,* that is, look intently at; by
implication to *regard* with pleasure, favor or care: - (cause to)
behold, consider, look (down), regard, have respect, see.

Once again, like the words "see" (*raah-rawaw*) and
"consider" (*biyn-bene*) that we have covered in Isaiah 52:15,
the implication involves much more than what the respective
English words can mean. "See:" râ'âh רָאָה,Strong's H7200 *raw-
aw'* a primitive root; to *see,* literally or figuratively (in numerous
applications, direct and implied, transitively, intransitively and
causatively): - advise self, appear, approve, behold, X certainly,
consider, discern, (make to) enjoy, have experience, gaze, take heed,
X indeed, X joyfully, lo, look, (on, one another, one on another,
one upon another, out, up, upon), mark, meet, X be near, perceive,
present, provide, regard, (have) respect, (fore-, cause to, let) see (-r,
-m, one another), shew (self), X sight of others, (e-) spy, stare, X
surely, X think, view, visions. "Consider:" bîyn בִּין Strong's H995
bene A primitive root; to *separate* mentally (or *distinguish*), that is,
(generally) *understand*: - attend, consider, be cunning, diligently,
direct, discern, eloquent, feel, inform, instruct, have intelligence,

know, look well to, mark, perceive, be prudent, regard, (can) skill (-ful), teach, think, (cause, make to, get, give, have) understand (-ing), view, (deal) wise (-ly, man).

It is my fervent conviction that the Shroud of Turin uniquely allows *all* to "see" and to "consider" the Messiah "pierced" and "crushed" in order to purchase the salvation of all Mankind. At one and the same time, the Shroud, with a precision that could only be orchestrated by Hashem, fulfills the time frames prophesied so many years ago. In a wicked and perverse generation that seems bent on removing every aspect of G-D from our daily lives, the Shroud offers scientific evidence that challenges unbelief and points to the detailed accuracy of the Word of G-D.

When both Gulf I and Gulf II wars broke out in Iraq, many preachers and pundits alike, pondered if this could be the start of Armageddon. However, as a pastor, I told my flock, in each case, that is was *not* the final prophesied conflict. Simply stated, the nations did not line up with the Scriptures. As this book nears completion, all the nations are in fact beginning to line up. At the top of the list, Persia (Iran) is bent on the destruction of Israel and has been a chief supporter of terrorists throughout the region. Gog-Magog (Russia) has begun to partner with Assyria (Syria) and has been invited by the Philistines (Palestinians) to help foster their stated aspirations to retake Jerusalem and "push Israel into the sea." Meanwhile, record numbers of Jewish people have made Aliyah to their re-established homeland. The Hebrew language has been restored: the only "dead" language ever reborn in the history of Mankind. Furthermore, the Most High has been revealing Himself to many of the sons of Abraham, even the offspring of the "bondwoman." Jews and Arabs alike have been receiving visitations that transform their lives as they accept the finished work of the Messiah at Calvary.

The bottom line for me at this point is that the Shroud of Turin is a "sign" whose time has come. A sign that fulfills much prophetic Scripture. A sign that leads those who truly "consider" it to "mourn" because of the price of their own sins. A sign confirming that a man spent time in the "belly of the earth" and left His image behind but no *body* to rot. A sign that points from the "*firstfruits of resurrection*" to the *first resurrection*! Not an idol to worship like the Asherah pole, but an image that allows us to *seek His face* in a very real way. An image that "startles and sprinkles," revealing the precious "*blood of expiation*" shed by the "spotless Lamb" slain from the foundation of the world. An image of a "*man*" whose regal serenity in spite of his painful and abused demise simply begs the question, "Who is this *man* and what is he to me?"

As the Jews anticipate the arrival of the Messiah, the Ishmaelites expect the Mahdi, and the world awaits Armageddon, *that very* question needs to be addressed in the heart and mind of every reader. At the end of the 1978 documentary "*The Silent Witness*," as the camera pans the image on the Shroud, the narrator states, "Only this much is certain, the Shroud of Turin is either the most unbelievable product of the mind and hand on record, or it is the most awesome and instructive relic of Jesus Christ in existence…Which is right? Who is he?"[38] In the intervening thirty-eight years, there is, in my humble opinion, virtually no evidence to support the theory of forgery, and overwhelming evidence in favor of authenticity. Over the years, when the evidence has been presented in many venues secular or religious, the results are the same: people's lives are changed for eternity by "seeing" for themselves the "*Suffering Servant*" foretold by the prophet Isaiah. Is today that time for you? Have you, the reader, settled the matter

---

38   John Walsh, as quoted from **The Silent Witness**, (London, Pyramid Films, 1978)

in your own heart and mind? That is the question I will address next.

WHO IS HE? AND WHAT IS HE TO ME?

Proverbs 30:4 "Who hath ascended up into heaven, or descended? Who hath gathered the wind in his fists? Who hath bound the waters in a garment? Who hath established all the ends of the earth? What *is* his name, and *what is his son's name*, if thou canst tell?"

Genesis 32:29–30 "And Jacob asked *him*, and said, *tell me, I pray thee, thy name*. And he said, wherefore *is* it *that* thou dost ask after my name? And he blessed him there. And Jacob called the name of the place Peniel: for *I have seen God face to face*, and my life is preserved."

Judges 13:18 "And the angel of the LORD said unto him, *Why askest thou thus after my name, seeing it is secret?*"

Judges 13:22 "And Manoah said unto his wife, we shall surely die, because *we have seen God.*"

Isaiah 7:14 "Therefore the Lord himself shall give you a sign; *Behold, a virgin shall conceive, and bear a son, and shall call his name Immanuel.*"

Isaiah 9:6 "For unto us a child is born, unto us a son is given: and the government shall be upon his shoulder: and *his name shall be called Wonderful, Counsellor, The mighty God, The everlasting Father, The Prince of Peace.*"

Jeremiah 23:6 "In his days Judah shall be saved, and Israel shall dwell safely: and this is his name whereby *he shall be called, THE LORD OUR RIGHTEOUSNESS.*"

(Emphasis added on all verses.)

The simple and most unavoidable fact about the Shroud of Turin is this: ***The Shroud is either the burial cloth of Yeshua of Nazareth, displaying all of the wounds which history records of His death, or it was an attempt to represent the burial cloth of Yeshua.*** It is most important to note that since science has ruled out human artifice of any kind, the Shroud ***IS*** an actual burial garment that ***MATCHES*** in every detail the passion, death, and burial of Yeshua.

Perhaps the very first scientist to identify the man of the Shroud as Yeshua was Yves DeLage, whose report met with such disdain by the French Academy of Sciences strictly *because* he claimed it was Yeshua. On his heels came the report of Pierre Barbet, "*A Doctor At Calvary*" an impressive virtual autopsy performed on early photographs along. Since that time, numerous scientists and theologians have added their opinion that the man of the Shroud is none other than the historical Yeshua.

When the late Bishop John A.T. Robinson, noted New Testament Scholar, liberal theologian and skeptic, was first confronted with the Shroud of Turin, he set out to disprove it based upon the Scriptures alone. After a detailed study however, he made the following astounding statement at the 1977 U.S. Conference of Research on the Shroud of Turin: *It is (an image) of the dead Jesus (Yeshua)...*vivid and majestic... *Yet if in the recognition of the face and hands and the feet and all the other wounds, we, like those who knew him best, are led to say, "It is the Lord!"* (John 21:7), then perhaps *we may have to learn to count ourselves among those who have "seen and believed:* (John 20:29). But that, as St. John makes clear, brings with it no special blessing (but) rather special responsibility."[39]

> John 21:7 "Therefore the disciple whom Yeshua loved said to Peter, "It's the Lord!" When Simon Peter heard that it was the Lord, he tied his outer garment around himself—for he was stripped down for the work—and threw himself into the sea." TLV

> John 20:29 "Yeshua said to him, "Because you have seen Me, you have believed? Blessed are the ones who have not seen and yet have believed!"" TLV

---

39   Rt. Reverend John A. T. Robinson, **The Shroud of Turin and the Graveclothes of the Gospels: Proceedings of the 1977 U.S. Conference of Research on The Shroud of Turin**, (New York: Holy Shroud Guild), p.30

When the reports of that conference were assembled, it was my privilege to compile and edit them into an official Proceedings. Those Proceedings were presented to the Centro Di Sindonologie in Turin, Italy, and played a key role in getting the door open for the research we conducted one year later in 1978. Keep in mind everything we had accomplished to that point in time was based solely on photographs! Yet we were able to establish several very significant characteristics of the Shroud that have stood the test of time: 1) three-dimensionality 2) non-directionality and 3) cloth-body distance correlation with image intensity. Exciting finds indeed, however then as now there is no known test to establish the identity of the man of the Shroud. In spite of which, one of the most noted skeptics in Christendom of our time identified the man as Yeshua and reportedly had a true change of heart where faith is concerned.

As many of us have stated over the intervening thirty-nine years, the answer to *that* question remains in the realm of faith. However, it has been my experience in my spiritual life that *faith*, contrary to popular opinion, is not *blind*. As Rabbi Paul points out, the creation itself shouts "Creator!"

> Romans 1:17–20 "For therein is the righteousness of God revealed from faith to faith: as it is written, *the just shall live by faith.* For the wrath of God is revealed from heaven against all ungodliness and unrighteousness of men. In unrighteousness they suppress the truth, because what can be known about God is plain to them—for God has shown it to them. *His invisible attributes—His eternal power and His divine nature—have been clearly seen ever since the creation of the world, being understood through the things*

that have been made. So people are without excuse—." TLV
(Emphasis added)

When I accepted Yeshua as Messiah I did not have a frontal
lobotomy! I checked my heart at the door of faith, not my brains.
Nor did I need the Shroud for my step of faith. The Shroud and
my interest in it came much later. On the other hand, my dear
friend and colleague "Dee" German, for many years, was proud
to be the self-proclaimed "resident agnostic" of STURP. After all,
it was his opinion from the start that G-D would certainly reveal
himself "through" science to one with a scientific "bent." Dee has
now joined the ranks of those who "saw and believed." For nearly
forty years most of the men and women of STURP have quietly
continued their research without much public fanfare thanks to
the ill-fated and now discredited C-14 dating fiasco. To date **ALL**
results have supported authenticity as the only logical conclusion
based on **ALL** the evidence. Quite frankly, I am convinced that
they all also believe the Shroud to be genuine.

So, if it is in fact Yeshua, what does that mean to every
human being? For years I have stated at every presentation that "the
Shroud is the most accurate depiction of the sufferings of Yeshua
Ha Mashiach you will ever see." Furthermore, I have added that
"You now know what it cost Yeshua to bear your sins, to go to the
Cross in your place and mine." People the world over have heard
the story of the Cross and the love of Yeshua for fallen Mankind.
But now in these last and evil days we are given an opportunity to
see with our own eyes what it truly was like.

When discussing this book with different people, a
prominent Messianic Rabbi, a believer whose father frankly helped
me along this path of research, I was told flatly, "The Jewish people
would have no interest in the Shroud." His father, who founded

one of the world's most influential Messianic groups, actually encouraged my research.[40] My conviction is that in the haze of misinformation about the Shroud, many dismiss it out of hand having never examined the facts. Strangely, the world's best and most up to date website on the Shroud was built and is maintained by Barrie Schwortz, a Jewish photographer and fellow member of STURP. Barrie recently completed his second visit to speak of the Shroud in London before the Ahmadiyya Muslim Community for their 50th Annual Gathering known as Jalsa Salana. That a Jewish researcher would be invited to present the evidence of Christ's burial garment to a large Muslim contingent is astounding evidence, in my opinion of the importance of this artifact to *all* mankind. The late Dr. Alan Adler who joined STURP after our journey to Turin made the vital discovery that the blood on the Shroud is human. Another prominent Jewish member of STURP was the late Don Devan of the Jet Propulsion Laboratory, whose digital enhancement of the Shroud images was included in the Proceedings, and which were presented to the Italian authorities to open the door for the STURP testing. There are others of course, but my point being the Shroud is not only of interest to those of the Christian faith. Jews and even non-believers, when examining the facts honestly, are drawn into study of this enigmatic relic. In fact, my conviction is also that the Shroud was meant to bridge the gap between Christians and Jews that has been fostered for two thousand years in every wicked way imaginable. Rabbi Paul, in the same context we have already discussed before, says the Gentile believers and Jewish believers will be grafted together into the same olive tree.

---

40   a) Personal Conversation with Rabbi Chaim Urbach, 2015; b) Personal Conversation with Rabbi Eliezer Urbach, 1978

Romans 11:17–24 "And if some of the branches be broken off, and thou, being a wild olive tree, wert grafted in among them, and with them partakest of the root and fatness of the olive tree; Boast not against the branches. But if thou boast, thou bearest not the root, but the root thee. Thou wilt say then, The branches were broken off, that I might be graffed in. Well; because of unbelief they were broken off, and thou standest by faith. Be not highminded, but fear: For if God spared not the natural branches, *take heed* lest he also spare not thee. Behold therefore the goodness and severity of God: on them which fell, severity; but toward thee, goodness, if thou continue in *his* goodness: otherwise thou also shalt be cut off. And they also, if they abide not still in unbelief, shall be graffed in: for God is able to graff them in again. For if thou wert cut out of the olive tree which is wild by nature, and wert graffed contrary to nature into a good olive tree: how much more shall these, which be the natural *branches*, be graffed into their own olive tree?"

The Mystery of Israel's Salvation

Romans 11:25–26 "For I would not, brethren, that ye should be ignorant of this mystery, lest ye should be wise in your conceits; that the blindness in part is happened to Israel, until the fullness of the Gentiles be come in. And so all Israel shall be saved: as it is written, There shall come out of Sion the Deliverer, and shall turn away ungodliness from Jacob:"

Once again, may I appeal to the Berean among you? Doesn't this confirm another prophecy from the Tanach? The prophet Ezekiel, was shown the valley of dry bones, and was given the prophecy, not only concerning the return of the Jews to their homeland, but a promise of resurrection and salvation.

> Ezekiel 37:12–22 "Therefore prophesy and say unto them, Thus saith the Lord GOD: Behold, O my people, I will open your graves, and cause you to come up out of your graces, and bring you into the land of Israel. And ye shall know that I *am* the LORD, when I have opened your graves, O my people, and brought you up out of your graves, And shall put my spirit in you, and ye shall live, and I shall place you in your own land: then shall ye know that I the LORD have spoken *it*, and performed *it*, saith the LORD. The word of the LORD came again unto me, saying, Moreover, thou son of man, take thee one stick, and write upon it, For Judah, and for the children of Israel his companions: then take another stick, and write upon it, For Joseph, the stick of Ephraim, and *for* all the house of Israel his companions: And join them one to another into one stick; and they shall become one in thine hand. And when the children of thy people shall speak unto thee, saying, Wilt thou not shew us what thou *meanest* by these? Say unto them, Thus saith the Lord GOD; Behold, I will take the stick of Joseph, which *is* in the hand of Ephraim, and the tribes of Israel his fellows, and will put them with him, *even* with the stick of Judah, and make them one stick, and they shall be one in mine hand. And the sticks whereon thou writest shall be in thine hand before their eyes. And say unto them, Thus saith the Lord GOD; Behold, I will take the children of Israel from among the heathen, whither they be gone, and will gather them on every side, and bring them into their own land: And I will

make them one nation in the land upon the mountains of Israel; and one king shall be king to them all: and they shall be no more two nations, neither shall they be divided into two kingdoms any more at all:"

Ephraim, son of Joseph, was born to a daughter of Egypt! Could that not represent the Gentile believers being grafted into the olive tree? Especially true, I suggest, when we are once again talking of a time when Judah (the Jews) have been restored to their homeland and have had Hashem "breathe" life into them again through the "mouth of the prophet!" Furthermore, Messianic, Orthodox, Reformed and secular Jews have been, in our time, restored to their own land.

Let me sum things up this way: If the Shroud of Turin is indeed, as I and many others have come to believe, the actually burial cloth of Yeshua of Nazareth, then it is for certain an image of the crucified Lamb of G-D who takes away the sin of the world. As such then, He is, to all who acknowledge these facts, both Savior and Lord.

We again turn to Rabbi Paul who, when writing to the Hebrews, his own beloved people, penned the following:

The Supremacy of God's Son

Hebrews 1:1–8 "At many times and in many ways, God spoke long ago to the fathers through the prophets. Hath in these last days spoken unto us by *his* Son, whom he hath appointed heir of all things, by whom also he made the worlds; who being the brightness of *his* glory, and the express image of his person, and upholding all things by the word of his power, when he had by himself purged our sins, sat down on the right hand of the Majesty on high; being made so much better than the angels, as he hath by inheritance obtained a more excellent name than they. For unto which of the angels said he at any time, Thou art my Son, this day have I begotten thee? And again, I will be to him a Father, and he shall be to me a Son? And again, when he bringeth in the first begotten into the world, he saith, and let all the angels of God worship him. And of the angels he saith, Who maketh his angels spirits, and his ministers a flame of fire. But unto the Son *he saith*, Thy throne, O God, *is* forever and ever: a scepter of righteousness *is* the scepter of thy kingdom..."

Hebrews 2:1–3 "Therefore we ought to give the more earnest heed to the things which we have heard, lest at any time we should let *them* slip. For if the word spoken by angels was stedfast, and every transgression and disobedience received a just recompense of reward; How shall we escape, if we neglect so great salvation; which at the first began to be spoken by the Lord, and was confirmed unto us by them that heard *him*;"

Yeshua foretold His own death on the Cross. He also confirmed, not only that He was sent to the "lost sheep of the house of Israel," but also that He would be rejected by that very generation to whom He was sent.

Luke 17:25 "But first must he suffer many things, and be rejected of this generation."

The good news is that, in that same message, Yeshua also foretold the generation in which we now live. In our generation, that "rejection," that "neglect" of the "great salvation" of our G-D still exists, but is now being overturned by the witness of those, who in love, take the good news to the "Jew first and also to the Gentile."

Romans 1:16 "For I am not ashamed of the Good News, for it is the power of God for salvation to everyone who trusts—to the Jew first and also to the Greek (Gentile)." TLV

That very Scripture was the foundational Scripture for our ministry and our logo has always included the Magen David and the Torah Scroll. That was the leading that Hashem placed on my heart. We also began to teach all of the Jewish Feast days, and though it was not popular, instituted a regular Sabbath service. My dear friend Eddie Santoro, who graciously allowed me to share the Shroud at his Messianic congregation in New York, told me, "Ken, you have a Jewish heart."[41]

When this book finally began to take form on paper and not just in my mind, my daughter Jejchelle made a startling discovery on Ancestry.com. It appears that my maternal grandfather (who passed away just before I was born) was an Ethiopian Jew. That possibility alone might explain many things. Why was his given name, as well as his siblings and other family members, taken from the Tanach: Emmanuel, Rachel, Rebecca, Leah? While we are still doing our due diligence and research, the thought occurs: like so many others before me, could that part of my heritage have been hidden in the plan of G-D so that at the right time I could bring

---

41   Personal Conversation with Rev. Eddie Santoro, 1995

forth the truth to my own mishpacha? Perhaps that question will not be answered satisfactorily any time soon, but wouldn't it be like the Lord to do something exactly like that to bring forth His Word of promise?!

By now you have been shown all the facts necessary to make a quality decision on your own concerning Yeshua. Look again at the suffering and death depicted on the Shroud of Turin. Read again the prophetic Word of Hashem concerning His suffering servant. Let your eyes be opened by the facts rather than the traditions, theology and opinion of others. Search the Scriptures and even your own heart and choose what you will believe. Don't let anyone else decide for you! For the prophet Jeremiah declares that everyone, for themselves, shall know the Lord.

> Jeremiah 31:33–34 "But this *shall be* the covenant that I will make with the house of Israel; After those days, saith the LORD, I will put my law in their inward parts, and write it in their hearts; and I will be their God, and they shall be my people. And *they shall teach no more every man his neighbor, and every man his brother, saying, Know the LORD: for they shall all know me, from the least of them unto the greatest of them*, saith the LORD: for I will forgive their iniquity, and I will remember their sin no more." (Emphasis added)

This is the promise of Hashem to His people in these last days...a promise that does not negate nor destroy the law but rather fulfills it in every way.

Yeshua declared two pivotal truths to His followers:

John 5:39 "Search the scriptures; for in them ye think ye have eternal life: and they are they which testify of me."

Matthew 5:17–18 "Think not that I am come to destroy the law, or the prophets: I am not come to destroy, but to fulfill. For verily I say unto you, till heaven and earth pass, one jot or one tittle shall in no wise pass from the law, till all be fulfilled."

In this volume, I have endeavored to lay out before you the facts as I know them concerning Yeshua Ha Mashiach. However, don't even take my word for it. Ask the Lord for yourself. Invite Him today to reveal Himself to your heart in the atonement for your sins. Not just for a year or until another Day of Atonement comes around, but rather that your names may *be inscribed for life*.

Shalom Mishpacha

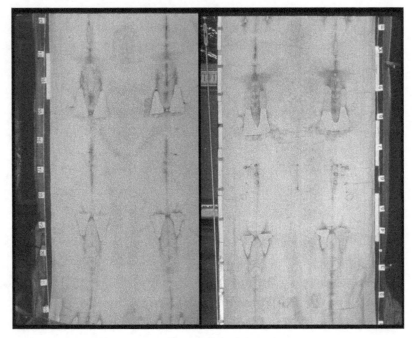

Turin Shroud

Precious Reader,

We thank our Blessed Heavenly Father for you, and we lift these words of prayer to Him on your behalf. We pray that all the knowledge and truth brought forth in this book has blessed you and touched your heart as never before; that it lead you to that new and wonderful place of relationship with Ha Shem, G-D the LORD.

Blessed and Most Holy Father, we lift our praise unto You, thanking You for Your Glory and Your Mercy and Your eternal lovingkindness. Let Your Word that has come forth in this work bless the heart, soul, mind and spirit of the person holding it right now. Your Word is truth and Your Heart for Israel, for Jerusalem, for the seed of Abraham is precious and filled with Light. Thank You for preserving Your people, O Father, and for raising them up for such a time as this.

We know, O LORD, how strange and even sometimes difficult it can be to be faced with what Your Word speaks about Your Son, Who He is and what He has wrought, but we know that Salvation belongs to the LORD, and by the Unity of Your Holy Spirit, we believe You for the salvation of this soul before You right now. Bless this reader, O G-D, and pour forth Your Spirit upon all flesh, even as the Prophet Joel declared. Let the trumpet be blown in Zion, even in the heart of this precious person here, and let the glory of the Lord be shining upon him or her. Bring Your son or daughter from afar, O Father G-D, to the place of the Name of the LORD, even to the Holy One of Israel. By Your Grace, bless this reader by Your mercies, Your most tender mercies that are new every morning and let the Day Star arise in their hearts. You have promised, O Blessed Father, that all Israel shall be saved, and out of Zion comes the One Who makes free, even for the reconciliation of the world that shall be life unto us all. Thank O

Ha Shem for forgiveness in the life and heart of this reader; that the anchor of hope and the faith of the Dear Son be born anew and afresh today in and for them!

We thank You in prayers and praise, O Father G-D, that the person reading this right now, come to dwell in Your secret place, O Most High, abiding under the shadow of the Almighty. Let them say of You, O LORD, that You indeed are now their refuge, their fortress, their Savior in Whom they shall trust. Bless them, O Ha Shem, deliver them, cover them; let them not fear or any of the things of the world that would try to hurt them or hold them back in any way. Let this person, right here, O LORD, be blessed in the knowledge of Your heavenly, warrior angels that are here to do Your will on their behalf. Let them know that there are righteous hearts before You, praying and believing for their safety, their hope and their future glory. We bless this person, this reader who has partaken of Your Word in a new and awesome way, even seeing evidence for the power of Your resurrection through Yeshua. Let them know, O Most High, that You have set Your love upon them. You have set Your love upon them! And they can set their love upon You, O Righteous Father, by the simplest action within that seed of faith You have given them. Hallelujah! May this reader come to know Your Name and begin to call upon You, not by any fleshly might or power, but by Your Holy Spirit.

We bless you, O Precious Reader, to be set on high even as the LORD our G-D, Creator of the Universe has declared by His Word, and that He show you…that He show you the greatness of His Glory, that He show you His Salvation, so preciously and powerfully wrought, here in the now and through eternity, His Salvation…just for you.

ACKNOWLEDGEMENTS

As always, thanks to Deborah Kublin for her artistic cover design and Frances Beauchamps for manuscript editing.

Bibliography

1. Summary of Official Statement, "**The Shroud of Turin Research Project, Inc. STURP.**" (Amston, CT 1981)
2. Carlton Coon, as quoted in Robert Wilcox, *Shroud*, (New York: Bantam Books, 1978) 130-133
3. Yves Delage, quoted by Ian Wilson, *The Shroud of Turin*, (New York: Doubleday, 1978) 20
4. Rabbi Solomon Ganzfried, *Code of Jewish Law*, trans. Hyman E. Goldin (New York: Hebrew Publishing Co., 1961) 89-91, 94-98
5. "Tefillin," 2016 http://www.JewishVirtualLibrary.org
6. Peter Stoner, *Science Speaks*, (Chicago: Moody Press 1944), Revised Online edition 2002 Chapter 3: http://sciencespeaks. dstoner.net/Christ_of_Prophecy.html#c9
7. "Jewish Holidays," 2016, http://www.chabad.org/holidays/ JewishNewYear/template_cdo/aid/568512/jewish/Why-do-we-read-the-Book-of-Jonah-onYomKippur.htm http:// www.chabad.org/holidays/JewishNewYear/template_cdo/ aid/430304/jewish/The-Story-of-Your-Life.htm

8. "Risen," http://sites.Sonypictures.com/risen/discanddigital Kevin Reynolds & Paul Aiello

9. Ian Wilson, *The Shroud of Turin*, (New York, Doubleday, 1978) 86–125

10. "Image of Edessa," 2016, Dr. Taylor Marshall, **How the Shroud of Turin Relates to the Ancient Image of Edessa,** - http://taylormarshall.com/?s=Image+of+Edessa&submit=Search pp.1–8

11. Kenneth Stevenson and Gary Habermas, **Verdict on the Shroud**, (Michigan: Servant Press, 1981) 26, 62

12. Peter Dembowski, **Sindon In The Old French Chronicle of Robert De Clari**, (Shroud Spectrum International, 2013), as cited on Shroud.com, http://www.shroud.com/pdfs/ssi02part5.pdf

13. Ian Wilson, *The Shroud of Turin*, (New York, Doubleday, 1978) 130–131 including photo inserts

14. Philip Dayvault, *The Keramion-Lost and Found*, (New York: Morgan James Pub., 2016) http://www.kermion502.com (visit directly)

15. Rev. Albert R. Dreisbach, *Thomas & the Hymn of the Pearl*, (Georgia: AICCST, 2000) 14

16. Rev. Albert R. Dreisbach, **Liturgical Clues to the Shroud's History**, (Georgia: AICSST, 1995)

17. "Linen," 2016, Hebrews Today, as cited by Zipporah Reshel, **Linen: The Preferred Fabric for Clothing of Healing, Healthy Living and Well Being**, (California 2006), http://www.zipporahsthimble.com/Linen_Info.html

18. Thomas De Wesselow, **The Sign: The Shroud of Turin and the Secret of the Resurrection**, (New York: Dutton, 2012) 326–327

19. William Stuart McBirnie, *The Search For The Twelve Apostles*, (Illinois, Tyndale House, 1973) 204

20. Thomas De Wesselow, *The Sign: The Shroud of Turin and the Secret of the Resurrection*, (New York: Dutton, 2012) 341–342

21. J. R. Watts, **Shroud Codes in the Bible**, (New York, Center for Biblical Cryptology), 2016

22. "In the Beginning,"2016, http://www.answersintheendtimes.com

23. Arno Lamm and Emile Vanbeckevoort, **Wake Up**, (Doorn Netherlands, Stichting Het Zoeklicht 2017), 56, 58, 232-233, 235

24. Kenneth Stevenson and Gary Habermas, *The Shroud and the Controversy*, (Tenn., Thomas Nelson, 1990) 214–225

25. Kenneth Stevenson and Gary Habermas, *The Shroud and the Controversy*, (Tenn., Thomas Nelson, 1990), 77

26. "Six Day War," Moishe Dayan, http://www.sixdaywar.org/content/ReunificationJerusalem.asp

27. Yitzchak Rabin: IBID

28. F.B. Meyer, *E-Sword Commentary*, (London Circa 1900?)

29. John Walsh, as quoted from **The Silent Witness**, (London, Pyramid Films, 1978)

30. Rt. Reverend John A. T. Robinson, *The Shroud of Turin and the Graveclothes of the Gospels: Proceedings of the 1977 U.S. Conference of Research on The Shroud of Turin*, (New York: Holy Shroud Guild), 30

Donor List

To my friends, family and loved ones, I offer my sincerest, heartfelt gratitude toward each of you for giving into this work. May the LORD our God by Yeshua Ha Mashiach bless you in abundance even as His Word says, "*Give, and it shall be given unto you; good measure; pressed down, and shaken together, and running over, shall men give into your bosom. For with the same measure that ye mete withal it shall be measured to you again.*" Luke 6:38

Jim Anderson
James and Marty Banfield
Alex and Frances Beauchamps
Paul Beauchamps
Gary Bone
Greg and Wanda Boone
Steven C. Briggs
Nicole Coleman
Ken Davis
Francis J. DeStafano

Doug and Robbie Fitzpatrick
Tom Fleming
Pastor Tony and Bridget Fontanelle
Edwin Franks
Michael Freeman
Robin H. Hanson
Ron Hindmarsh
Paul and Linda Jablonowski
Kathy Jennings
Emil and Deborah Kublin
Joseph G. Marino
Prophetess Nina Marie McElroy
Kris Mineau
Reverend Anita Saunders
Roy and Faith Sauzek
Gwendolyn Sealey
Ruurd Sieffers
Pierre St. Arnault
Eileen Stevenson
E. Adrian and Lexie Van Zelfden
Curt Stevens

"And, behold, I come quickly; and my reward is with me, to give every man according as his work shall be. I am Alpha and Omega, the beginning and the end, the first and the last. Blessed are they that do his commandments, that they may have right to the tree of life, and may enter in through the gates into the city."
Revelation 22:12-14

Morgan James
Speakers Group

www.TheMorganJamesSpeakersGroup.com

We connect Morgan James published
authors with live and online events
and audiences who will benefit
from their expertise.

Printed in the USA
CPSIA information can be obtained
at www.ICGtesting.com
JSHW022333140824
68134JS00019B/1459